EDU KIDS
P R E S S

GET FREE EXTRA STUFF!

Email us at

hello@edukidspress.com

Put "learn to write numbers" in the email subject line and we will send you free extra fun worksheets!

Find us on Instagram

This book belongs to:

Note to Parents

Fine motor skills are the foundation of early handwriting! Preschool- and kindergarten-aged children benefit from daily activities that develop these skills in fun and developmentally appropriate ways. Children need to first work on building up the motor readiness required to (a) firmly grasp a writing utensil, and (b) hold it steady while creating smooth strokes. This workbook focuses on developing these two skills, while also introducing numbers and lower case letters of the English alphabet for each number written out.

In addition to the activities in this workbook, consider trying the following with your young student:

Playing with finger puppets

Playing with tops to spin

Practice using a squeeze-trigger spray bottle to water plants

Practice using child-safe tweezers or tongs to pick up small items like pom-pons or cotton balls and place them in empty containers

Make necklaces out of Fruit Loops, Cheerios, or macaroni by stringing them on yarn

Let them play with cards, coins, or buttons on the floor and encourage your child to turn them over

Save your old greeting cards so your child can cut them up, using child-safe scissors; this thicker paper provides the resistance children need to build strength

Tracing and Writing Numbers

This section of the workbook will focus on combining strokes into numbers and strokes into lower case letters of the English alphabet. This will be done via tracing; each page provides multiple chances to trace each number as a word and as a numeral. The letters and numerals have arrows to guide where to start and in which direction the stroke should go.

It's not necessary to complete all pages in one sitting, although each page should be completed before going on to the next. The child should complete each page at their own pace and, ideally, with the encouragement and engagement of an adult.

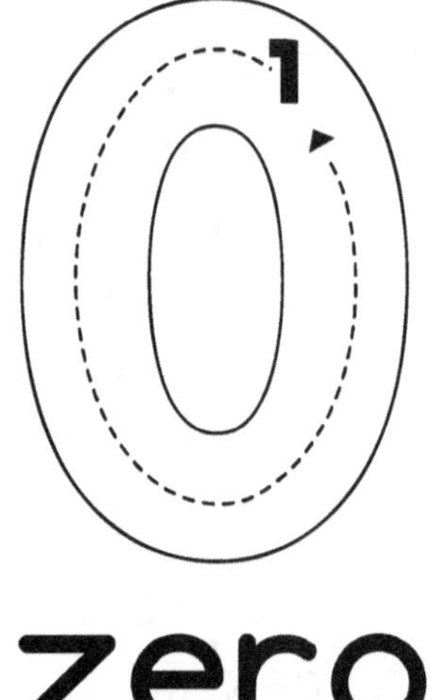

zero

How many eggs do you see in the bird's nest above? Write the number in where the arrow is pointing.

Trace the number below. Remember the direction of the arrow.

Trace the number below. Remember the direction of the arrow.

Write the number "zero" 6 times below. Remember the direction of the arrow.

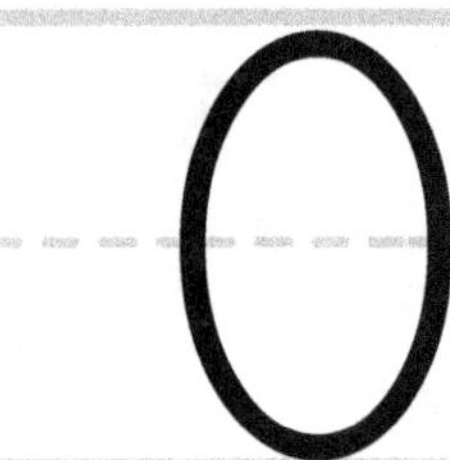

4	8	7	3	6	5	1	0
0	5	4	6	2	7	9	1
8	2	1	0	2	9	8	2
5	0	2	6	0	3	5	1
4	5	2	3	3	6	0	4

Circle all the **zeros** above.

How many fish do you see in the fishbowl?

Write your answer below!

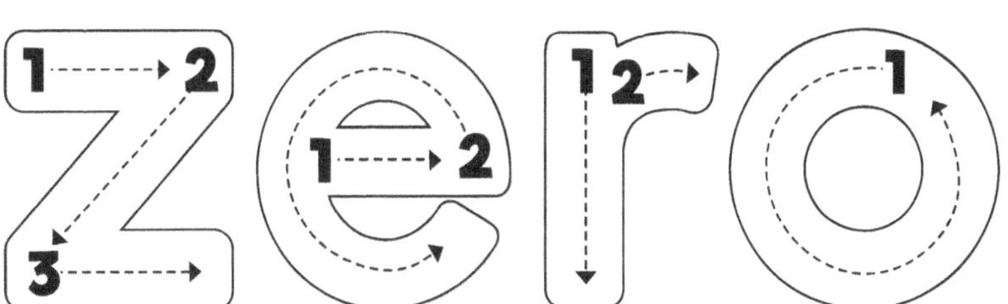

Trace the word zero below. Remember the direction of the arrow.

Write the word zero below.

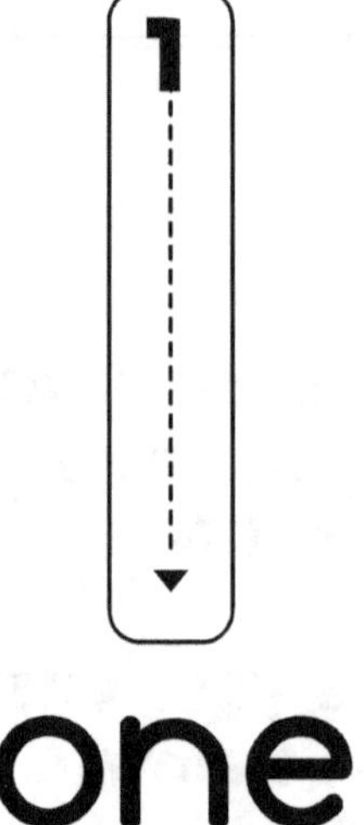

one

How many hippos do you see in the mud above? Write the number in where the arrow is pointing.

Trace the number below. Remember the direction of the arrow.

Trace the number below. Remember the direction of the arrow.

Write the number "one" 6 times below. Remember the direction of the arrow.

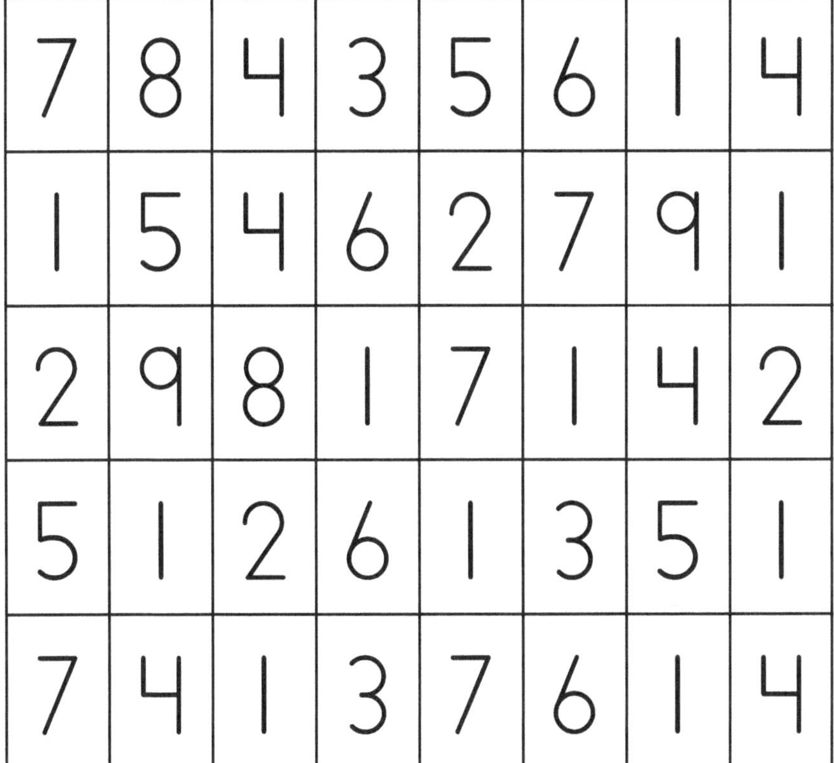

How many candles do you see on the cake?

Write your answer below!

Circle all the **ones** above.

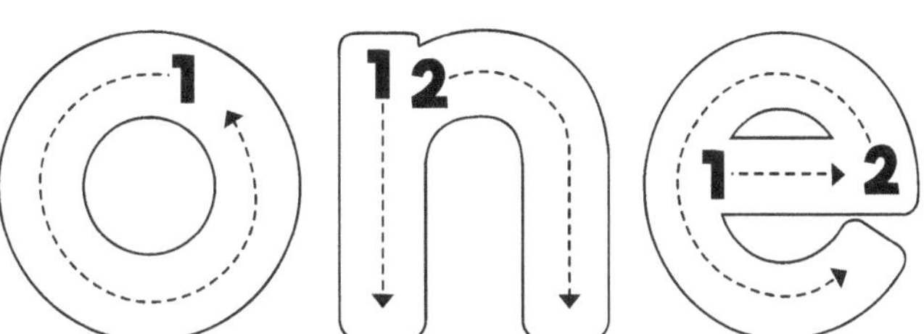

Trace the word one below. Remember the direction of the arrow.

Write the word one below.

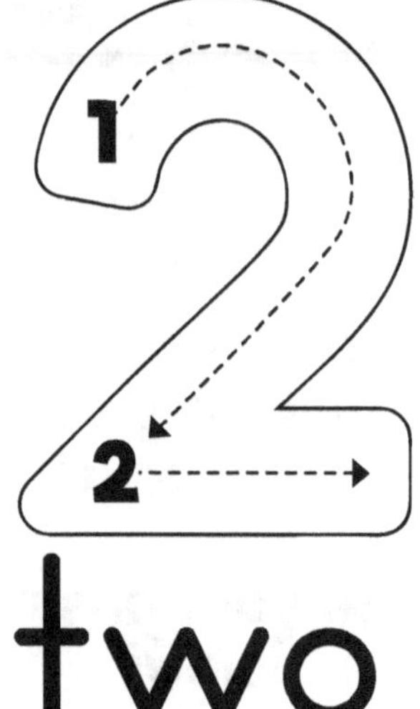

two

How many giraffes do you see in the mud above? Write the number in where the arrow is pointing.

Trace the number below. Remember the direction of the arrow.

2 2 2 2 2 2 2

Trace the number below. Remember the direction of the arrow.

2 2 2 2 2 2 2

Write the number "two" 6 times below. Remember the direction of the arrow.

2

6	5	2	3	1	2	3	8
2	4	6	9	7	1	1	2
7	1	8	2	4	2	2	9
1	3	2	6	5	1	5	2
2	6	1	4	2	4	7	4

Circle all the **twos** above.

How many apples do you see?

Write your answer below!

____

- - - - - - - - - - - - - -

____

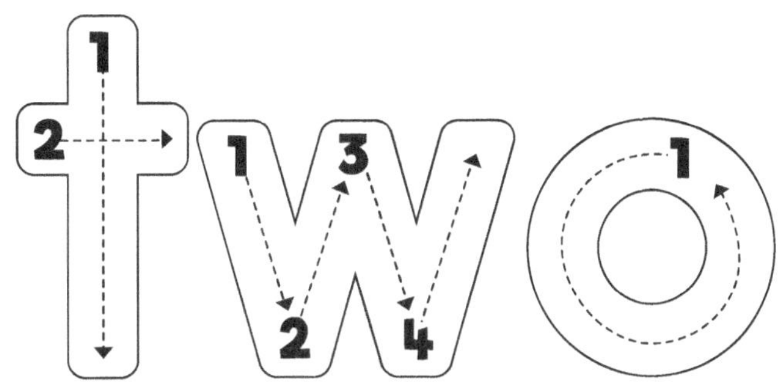

Trace the word two below. Remember the direction of the arrow.

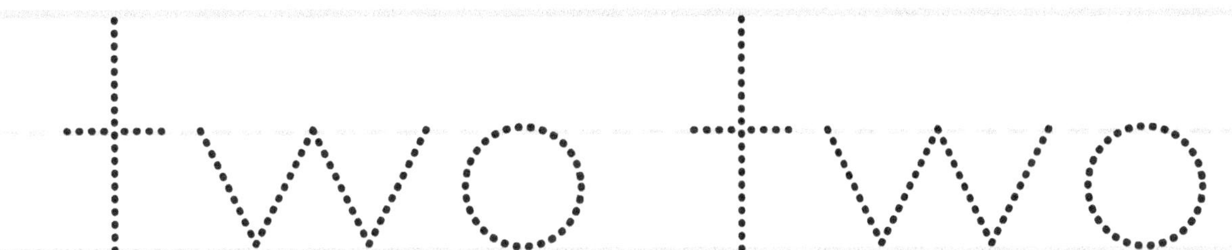

Write the word two below.

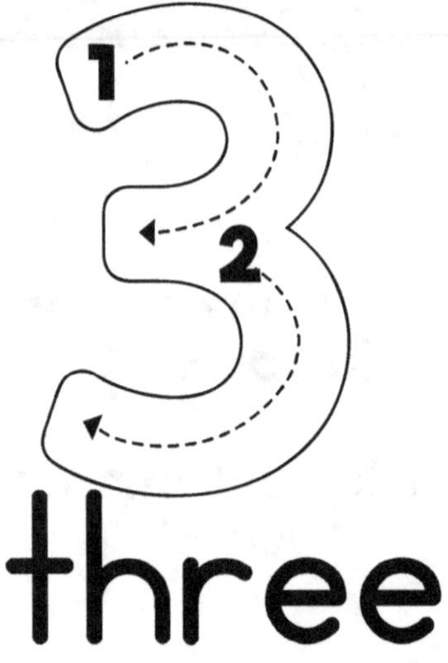

three

How many lions do you see in the mud above? Write the number in where the arrow is pointing.

Trace the number below. Remember the direction of the arrow.

3 3 3 3 3 3 3

Trace the number below. Remember the direction of the arrow.

3 3 3 3 3 3 3

Write the number "three" 6 times below. Remember the direction of the arrow.

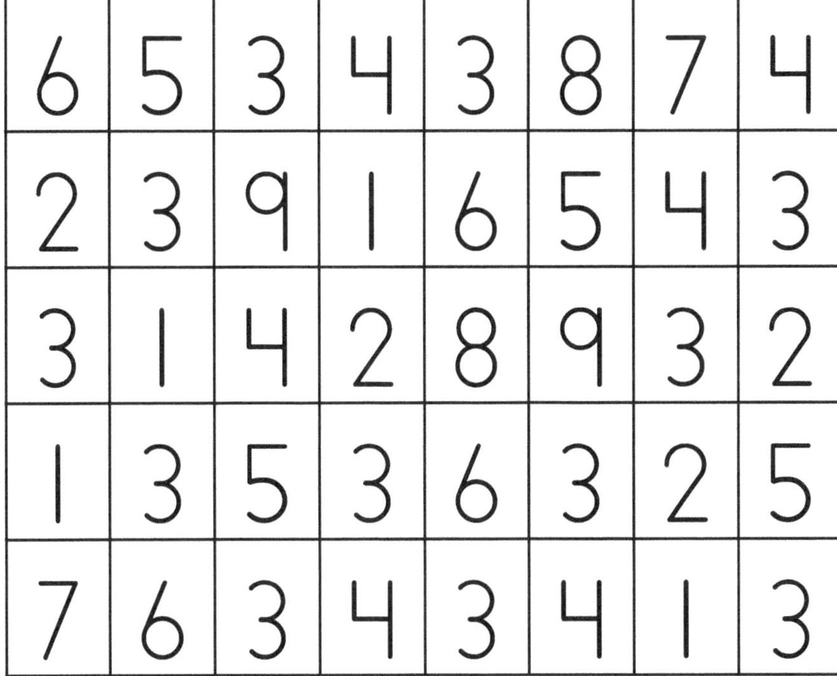

Circle all the **threes** above.

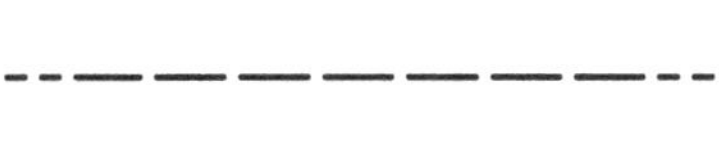

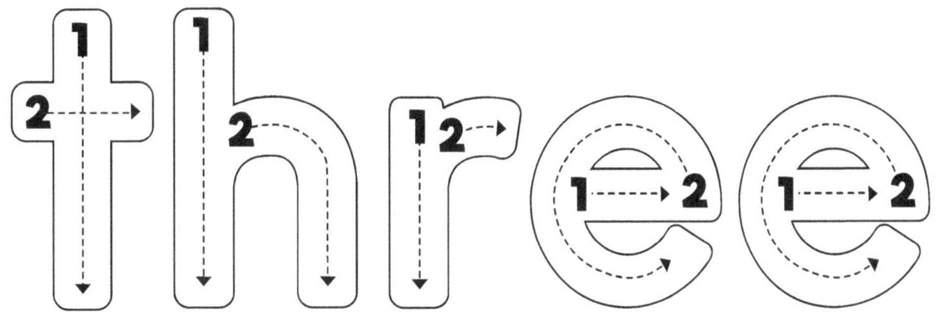

Trace the word three below. Remember the direction of the arrow.

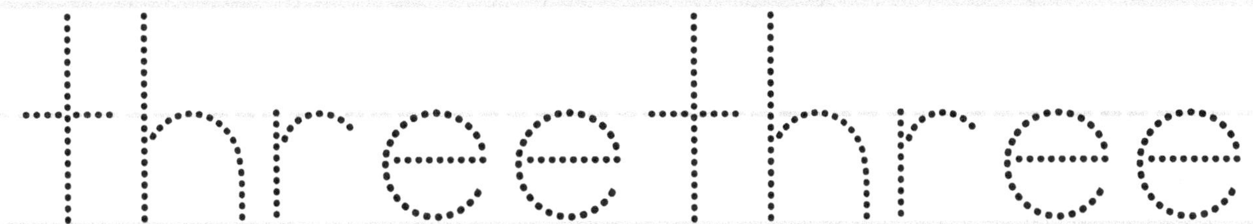

Write the word three below.

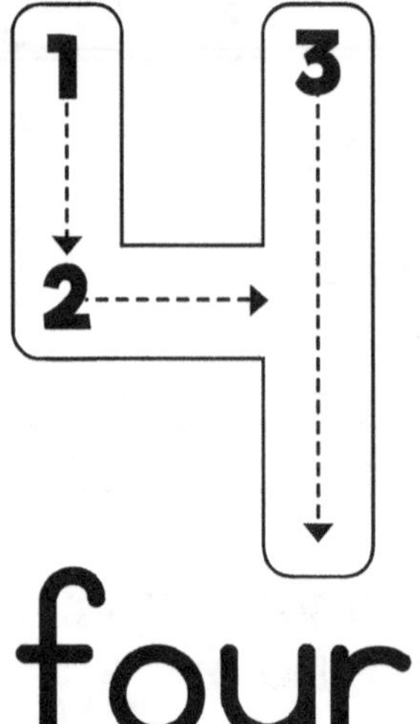

four

How many bears do you see in the mud above? Write the number in where the arrow is pointing.

Trace the number below. Remember the direction of the arrow.

Trace the number below. Remember the direction of the arrow.

Write the number "four" 6 times below. Remember the direction of the arrow.

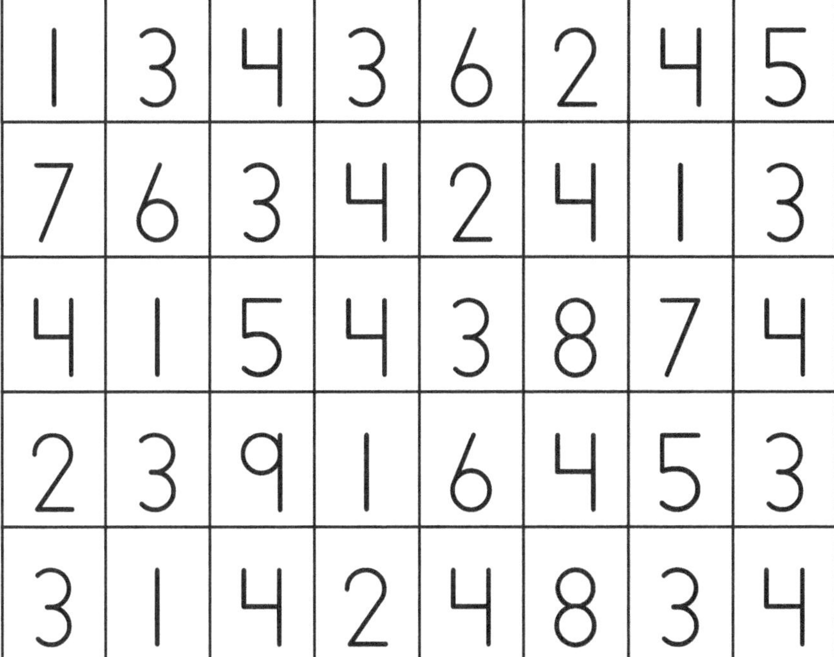

Circle all the **fours** above.

How many ice creams so you see?

Write your answer below!

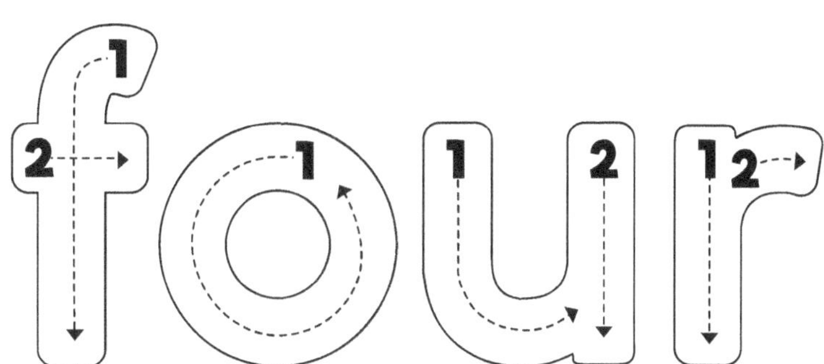

Trace the word four below. Remember the direction of the arrow.

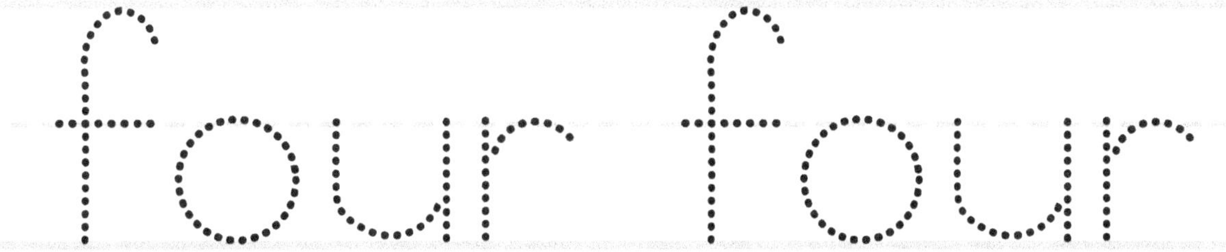

Write the word four below.

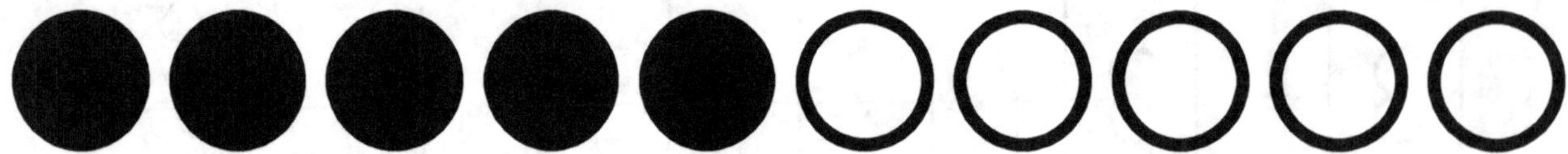

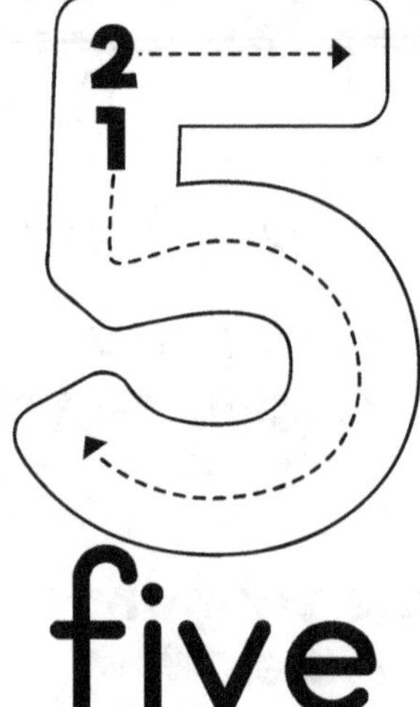

2
1

5
five

How many monkeys do you see swinging above? Write the number in where the arrow is pointing.

Trace the number below. Remember the direction of the arrow.

5 5 5 5 5 5 5

Trace the number below. Remember the direction of the arrow.

5 5 5 5 5 5 5

Write the number "five" 6 times below. Remember the direction of the arrow.

5

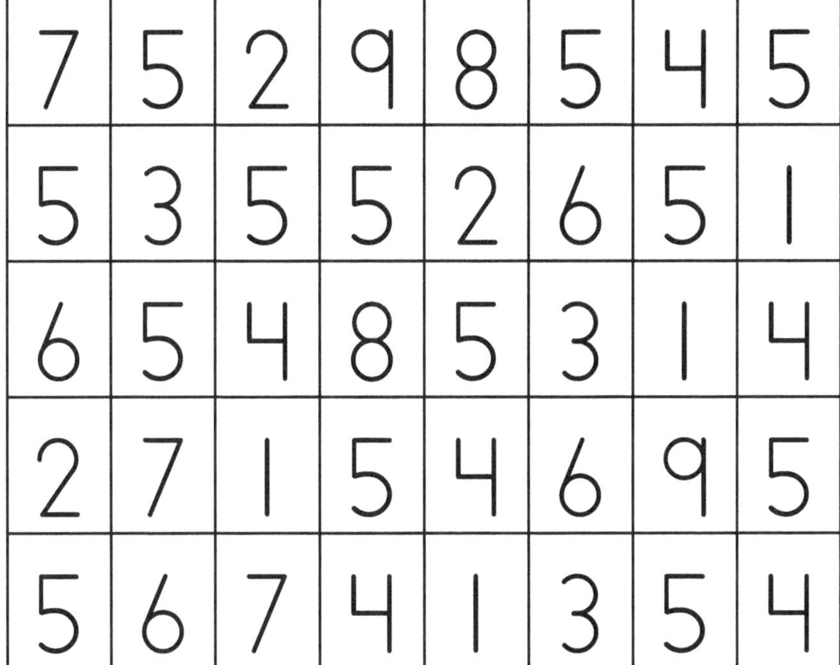

How many hearts do you see?

Write your answer below!

Circle all the **fives** above.

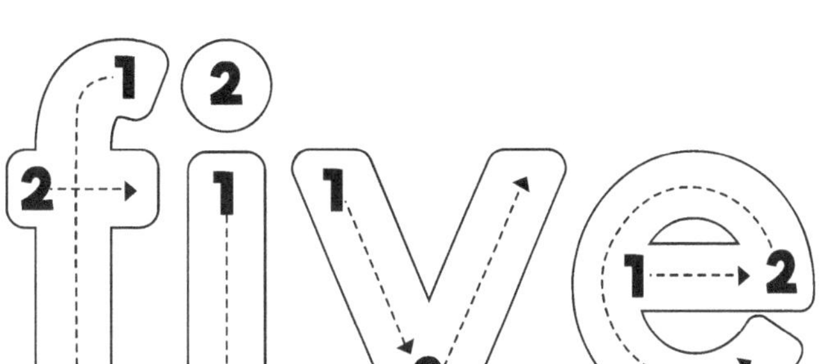

Trace the word five below. Remember the direction of the arrow.

Write the word five below.

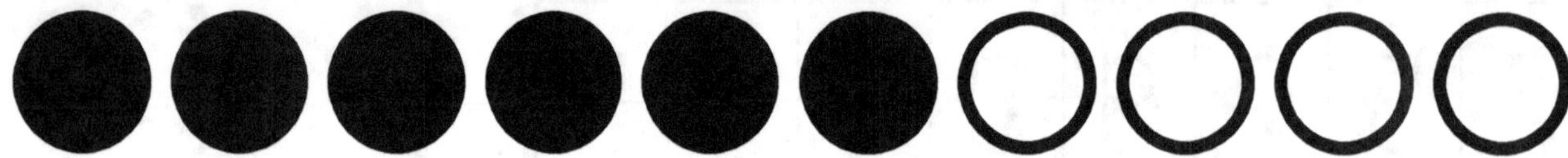

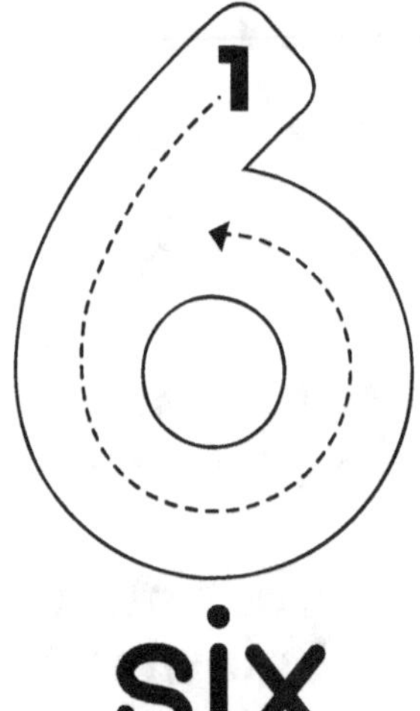

6
1
six

How many parrots do you see in the tree above? Write the number in where the arrow is pointing.

Trace the number below. Remember the direction of the arrow.

6 6 6 6 6 6 6

Trace the number below. Remember the direction of the arrow.

6 6 6 6 6 6 6

Write the number "six" 6 times below. Remember the direction of the arrow.

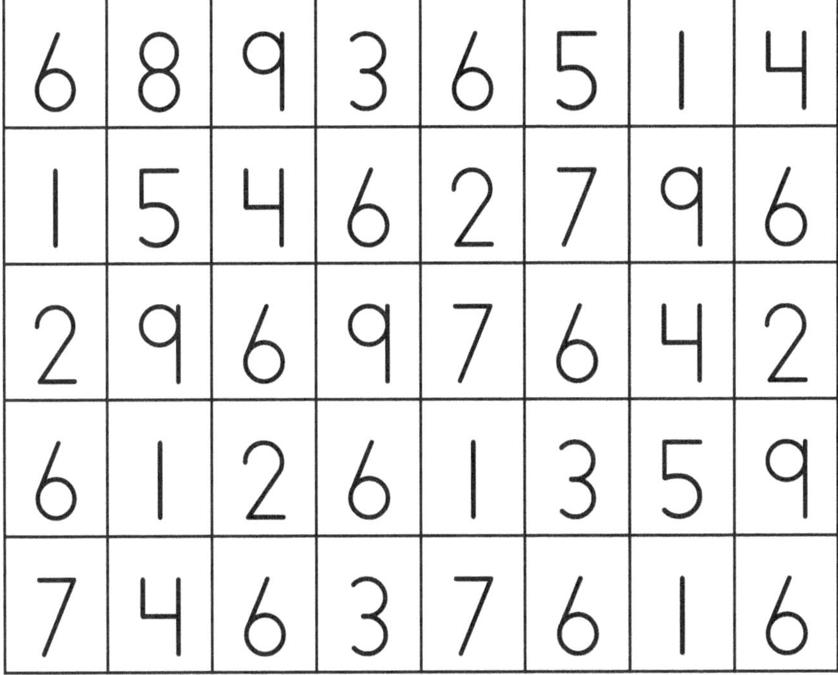

Circle all the **sixes** above.

How many clouds do you see?

Write your answer below!

Trace the word six below. Remember the direction of the arrow.

Write the word six below.

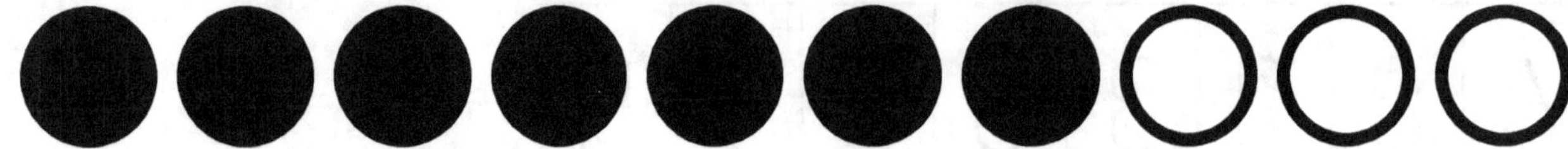

seven

How many turtles do you see in the mud above? Write the number in where the arrow is pointing.

Trace the number below. Remember the direction of the arrow.

Trace the number below. Remember the direction of the arrow.

Write the number "seven" 6 times below. Remember the direction of the arrow.

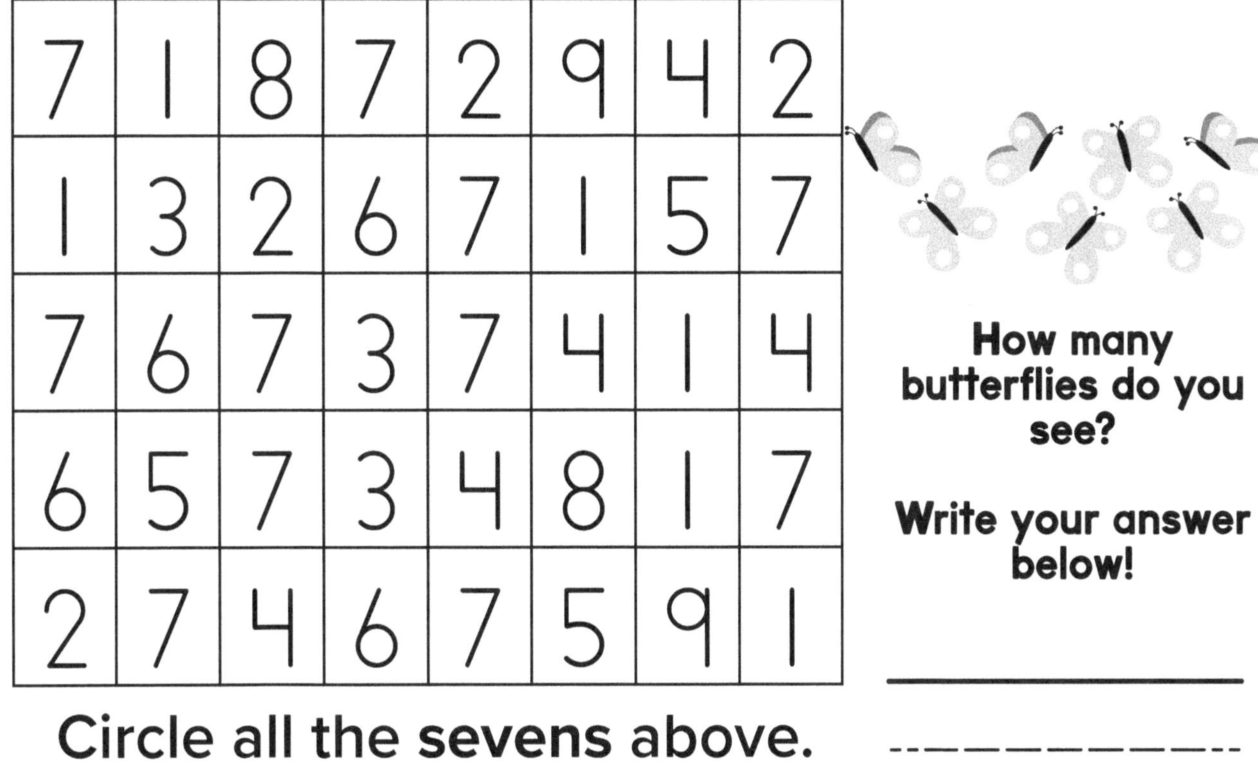

7	1	8	7	2	9	4	2
1	3	2	6	7	1	5	7
7	6	7	3	7	4	1	4
6	5	7	3	4	8	1	7
2	7	4	6	7	5	9	1

Circle all the sevens above.

How many butterflies do you see?

Write your answer below!

____

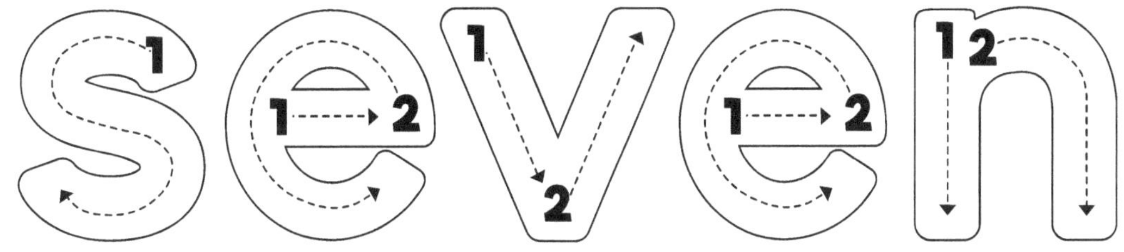

Trace the word seven below. Remember the direction of the arrow.

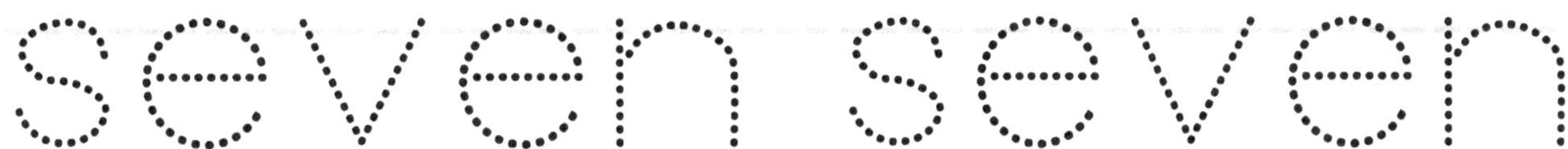

Write the word seven below.

eight

How many owls do you see above?
Write the number in where the arrow
is pointing.

Trace the number below. Remember the direction of the arrow.

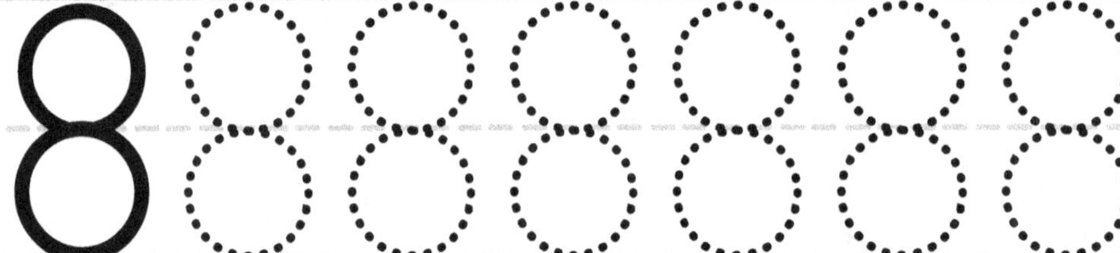

Trace the number below. Remember the direction of the arrow.

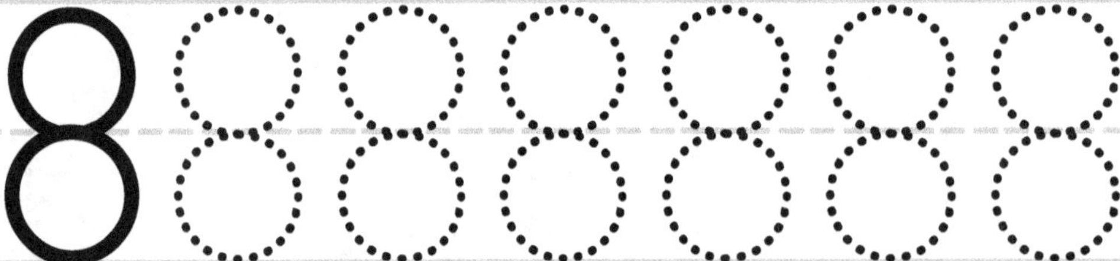

Write the number "eight" 6 times below. Remember the direction of the arrow.

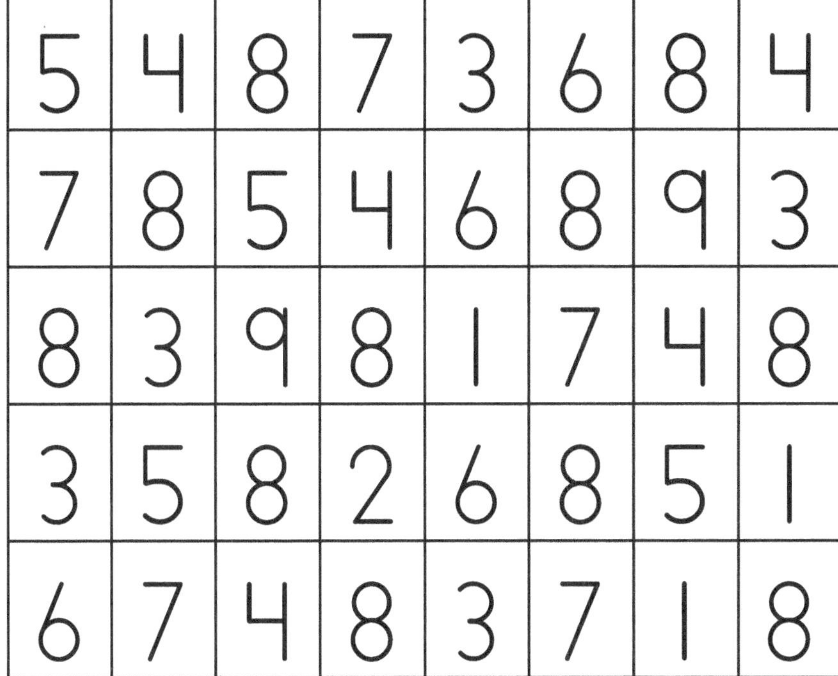

How many leaves do you see?

Write your answer below!

____

Circle all the eights above.

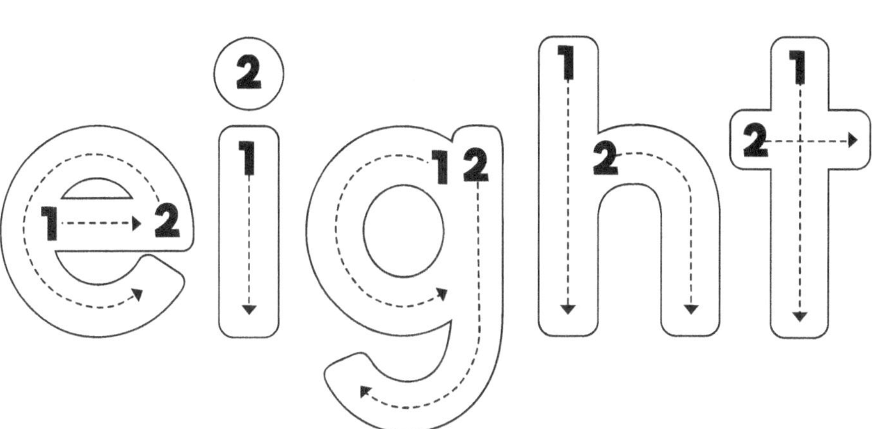

Trace the word eight below. Remember the direction of the arrow.

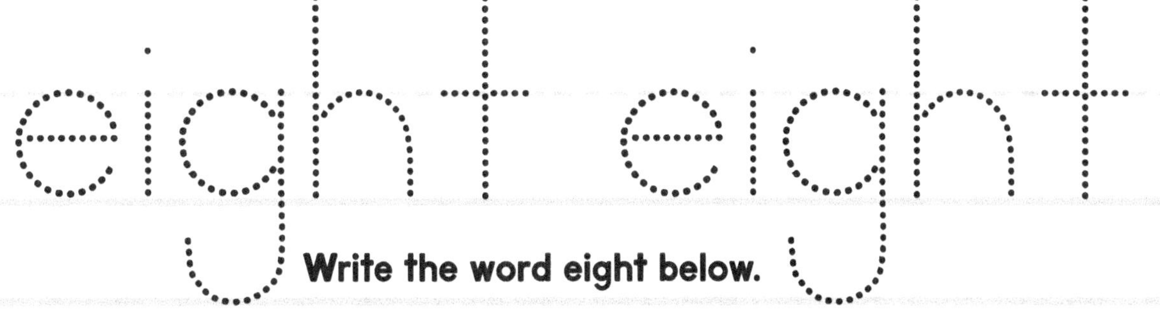

Write the word eight below.

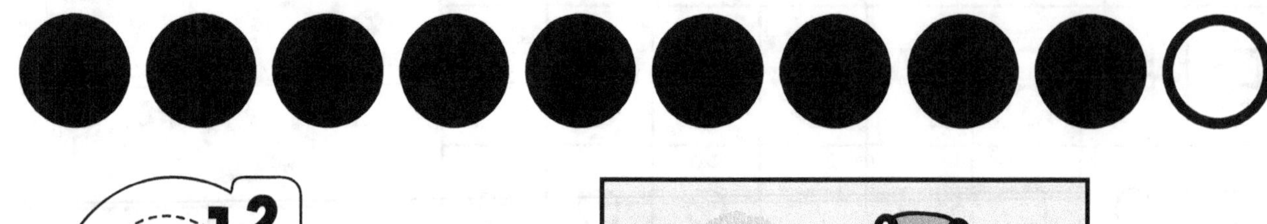

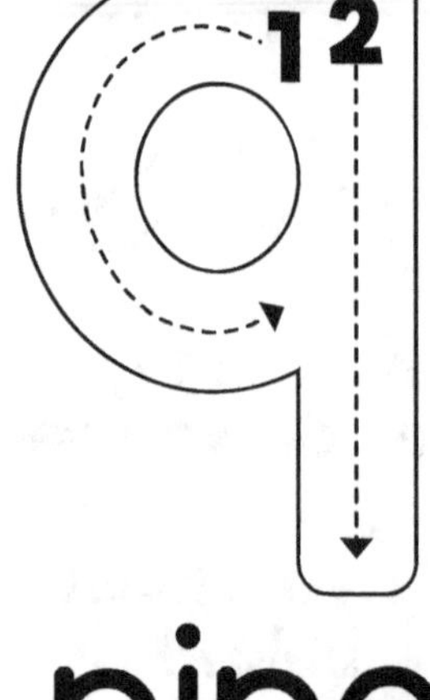

nine

How many frogs do you see in the water above? Write the number in where the arrow is pointing.

Trace the number below. Remember the direction of the arrow.

Trace the number below. Remember the direction of the arrow.

Write the number "nine" 6 times below. Remember the direction of the arrow.

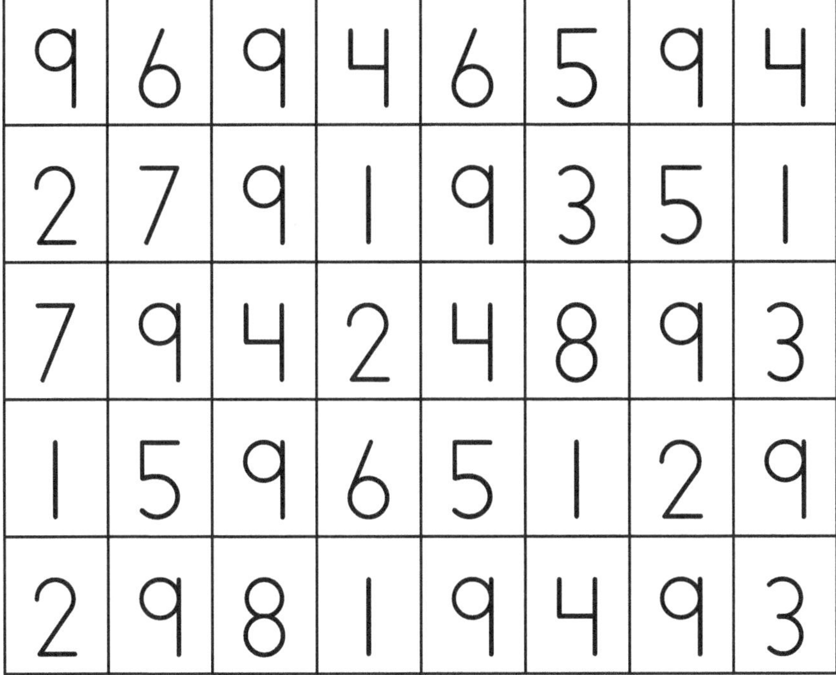

How many bees do you see?

Write your answer below!

Circle all the nines above.

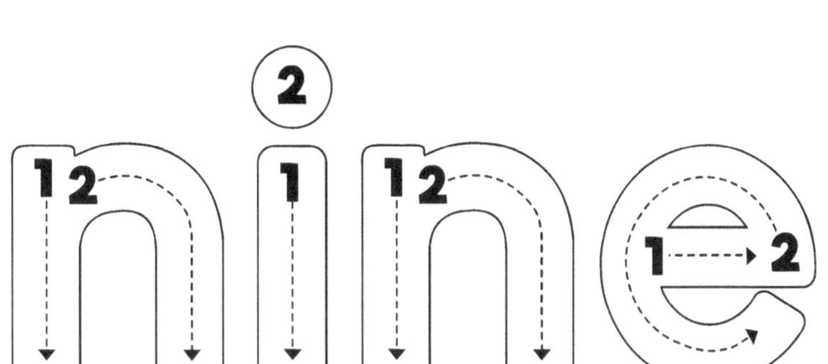

Trace the word nine below. Remember the direction of the arrow.

Write the word nine below.

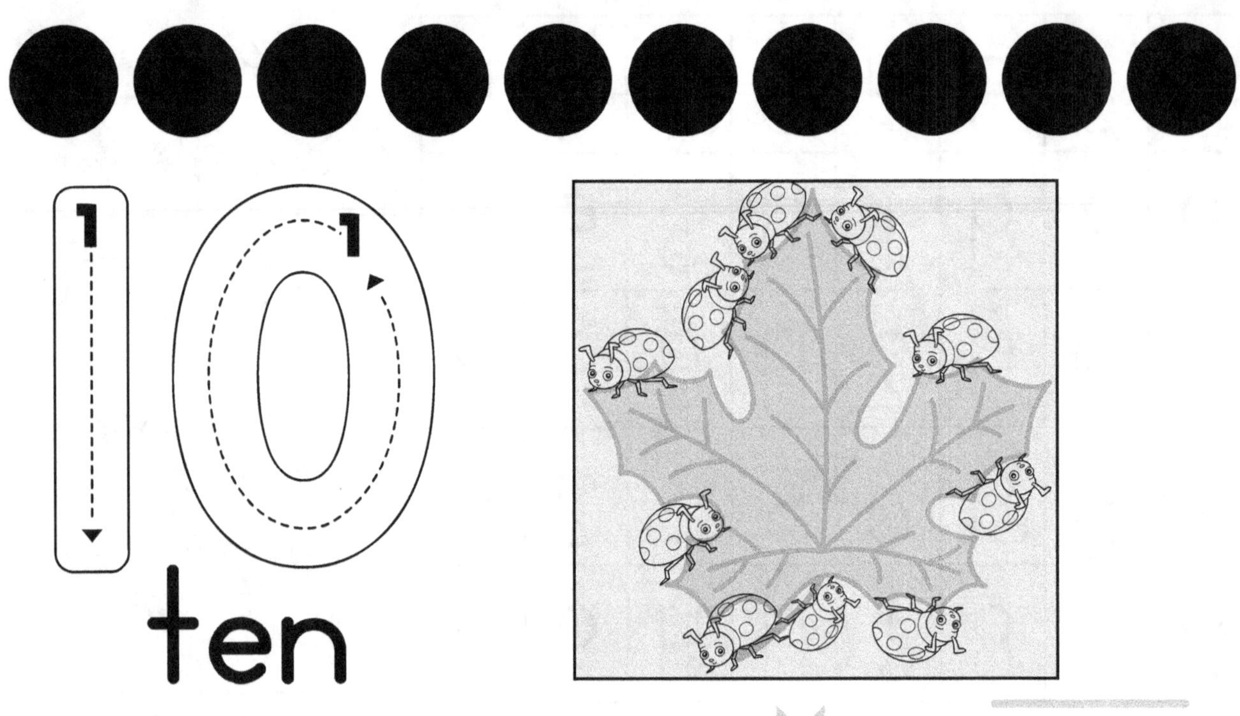

10
ten

How many ladybugs do you see on the leaf above? Write the number in where the arrow is pointing.

Trace the number below. Remember the direction of the arrow.

10 10 10 10 10 10

Trace the number below. Remember the direction of the arrow.

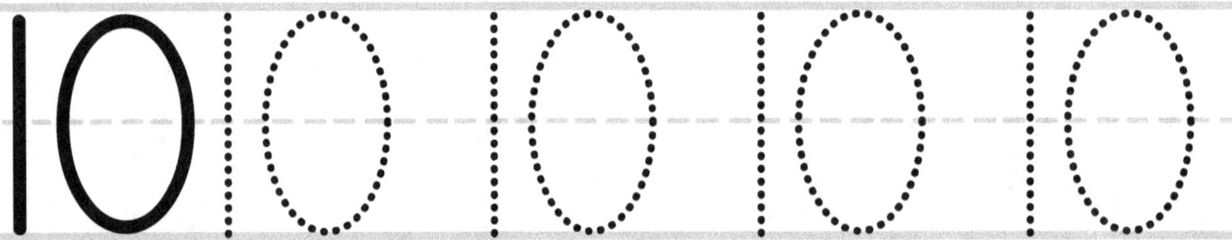

Write the number "ten" 4 times below. Remember the direction of the arrow.

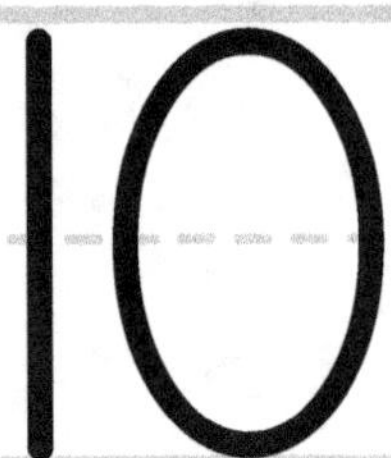

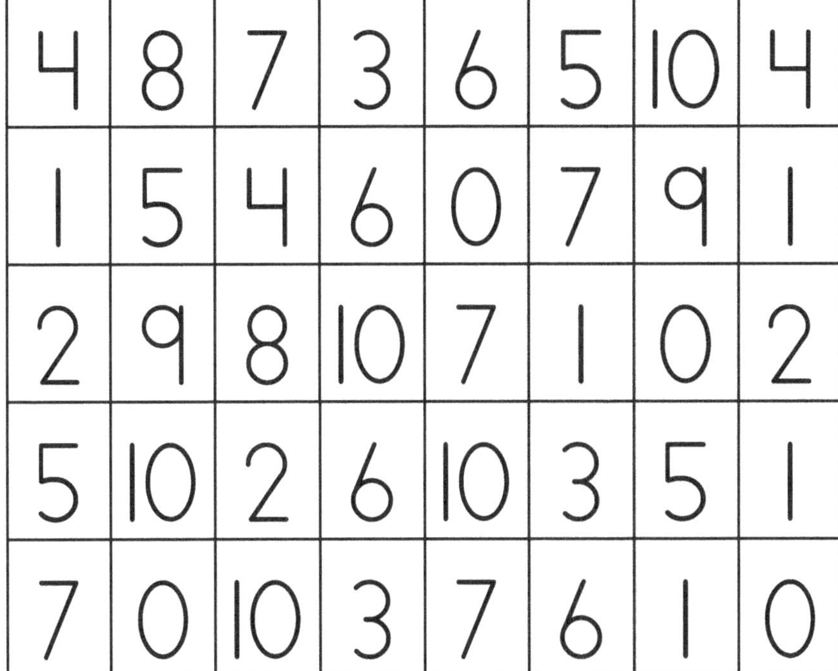

How many
stars do you see?

Write your answer
below!

Circle all the **tens** above.

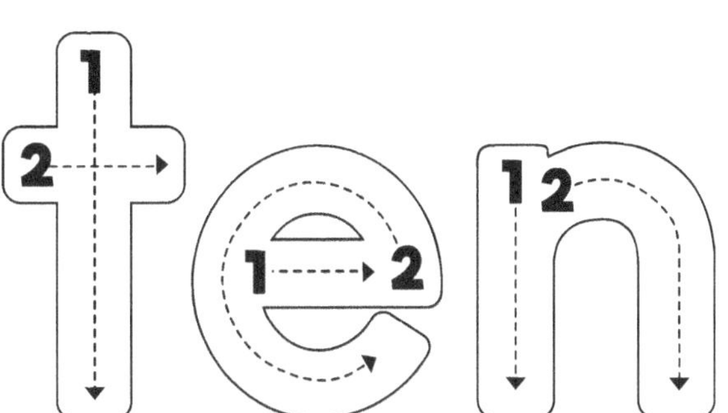

Trace the word ten below. Remember the direction of the arrow.

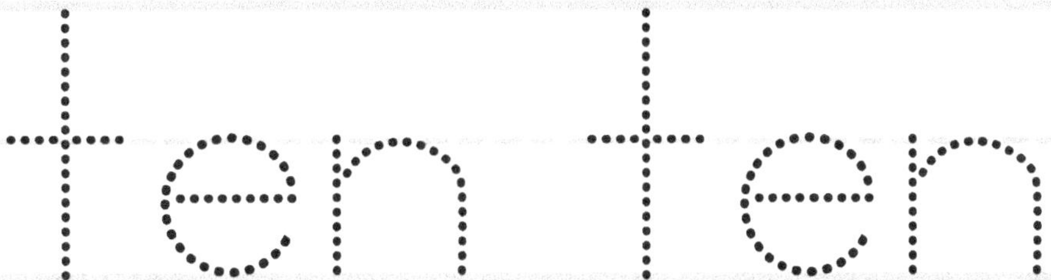

Write the word ten below.

Number review!

Count each domino and place the correct number in the dashed box, then write the number in the lined space.

0   zero

How many shapes

Count each type of shape and place the number of each shape type in the box at the right.

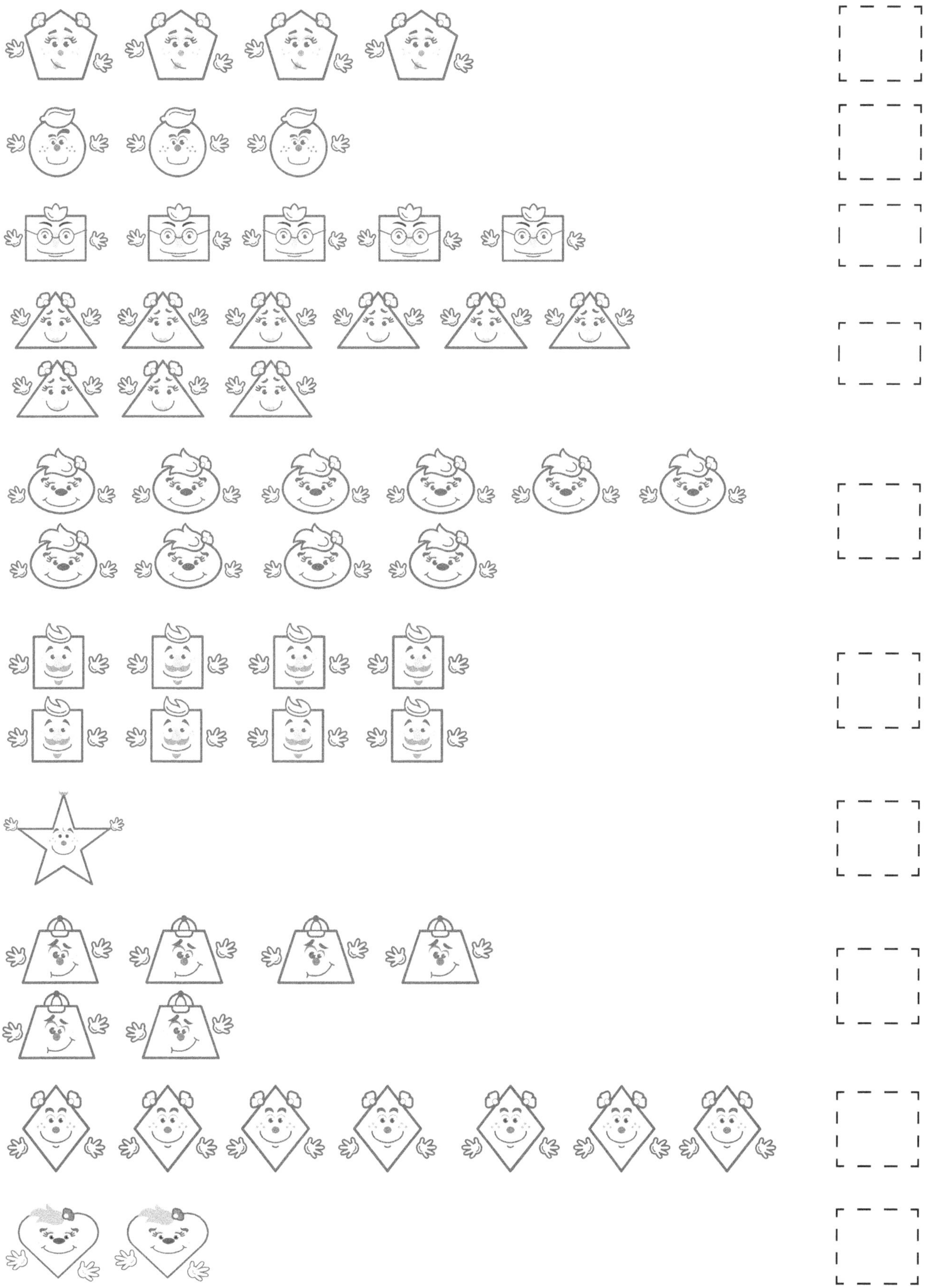

Find the number

Color in all the cells that have the number 0 to reveal a picture.

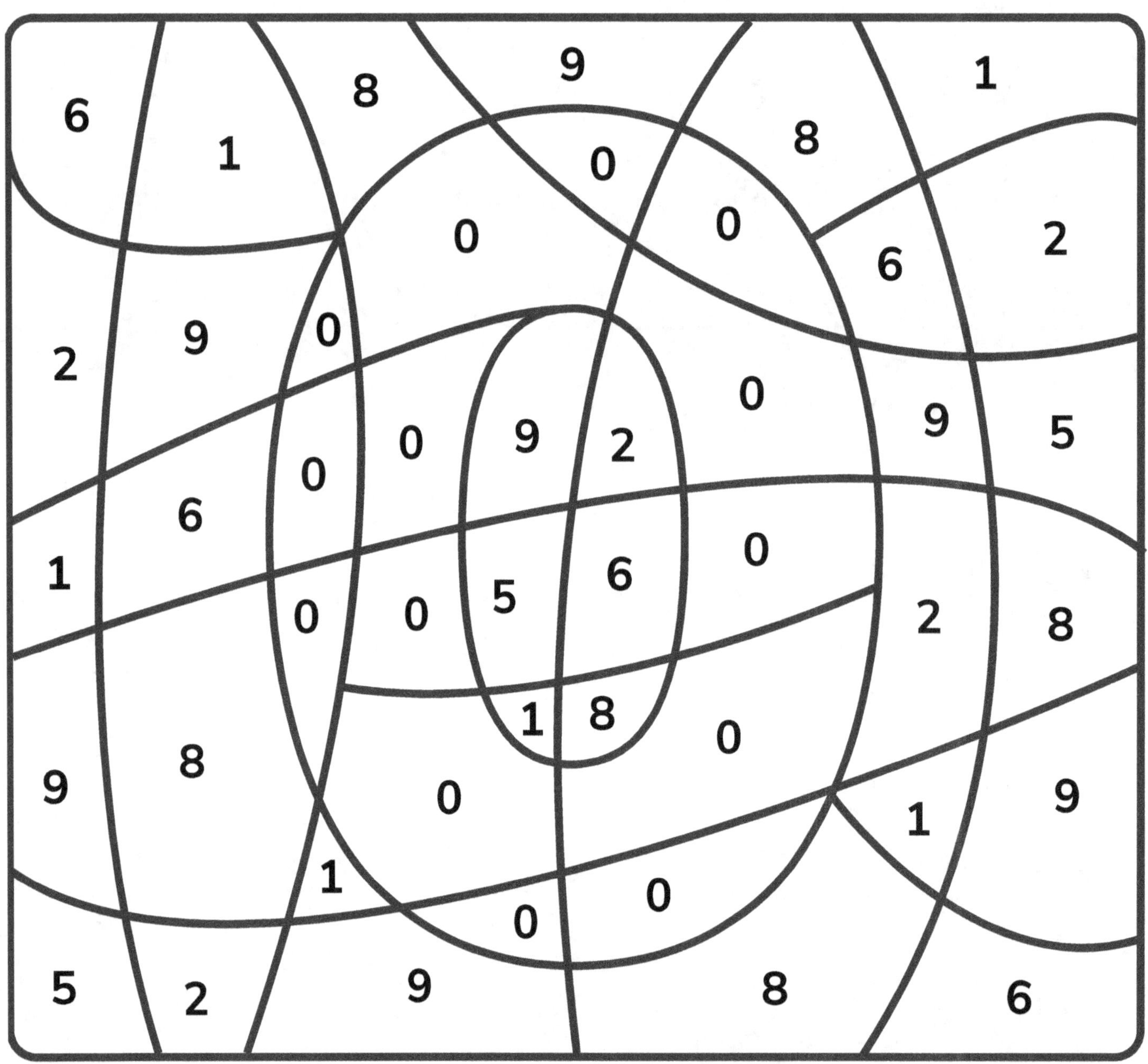

Place the number of the picture in the box below then write it out.

Find the number

Color in all the cells that have the number 7 to reveal a picture.

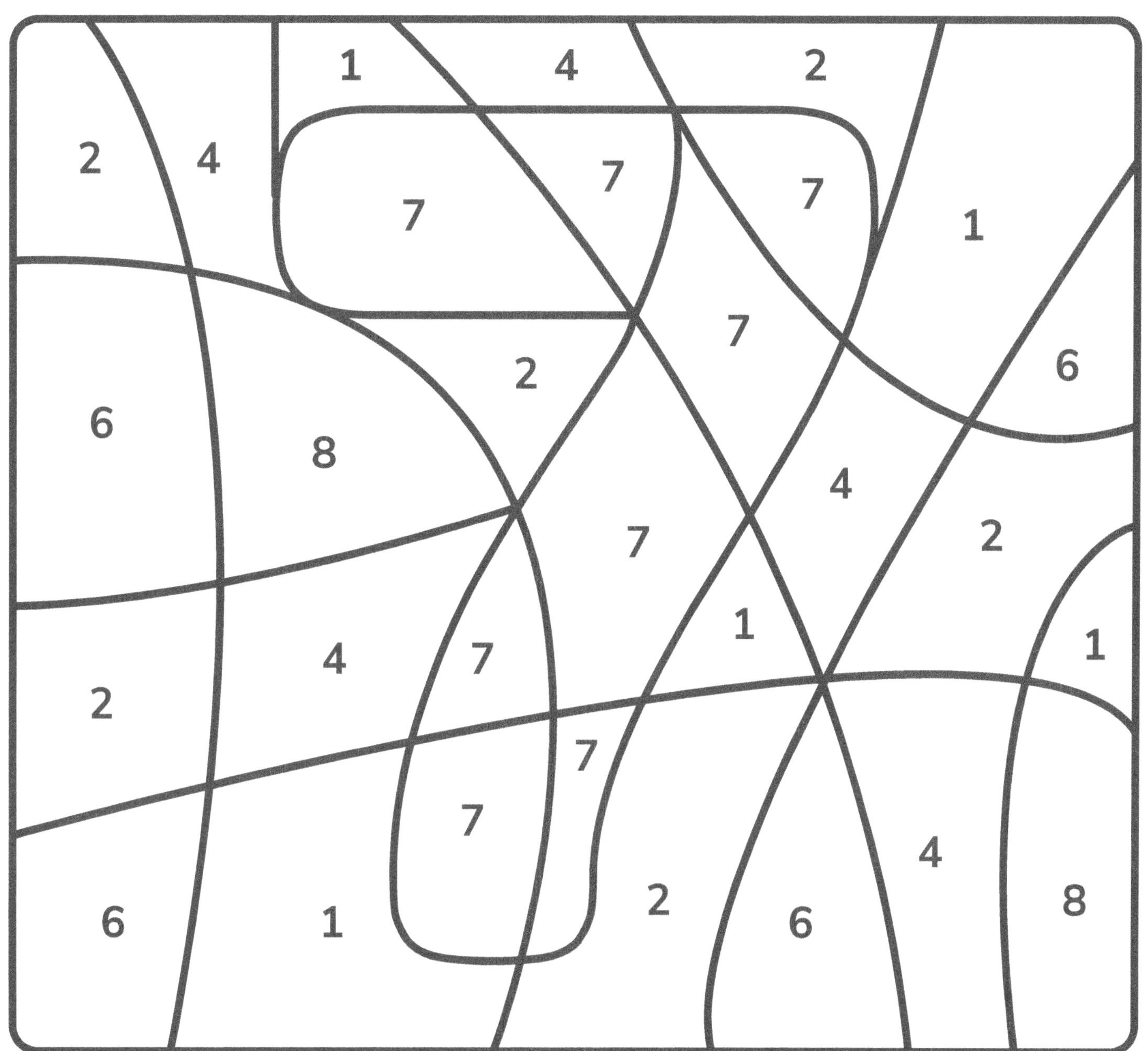

Place the number of the picture in the box below then write it out.

Find the number

Color in all the cells that have the number 2 to reveal a picture.

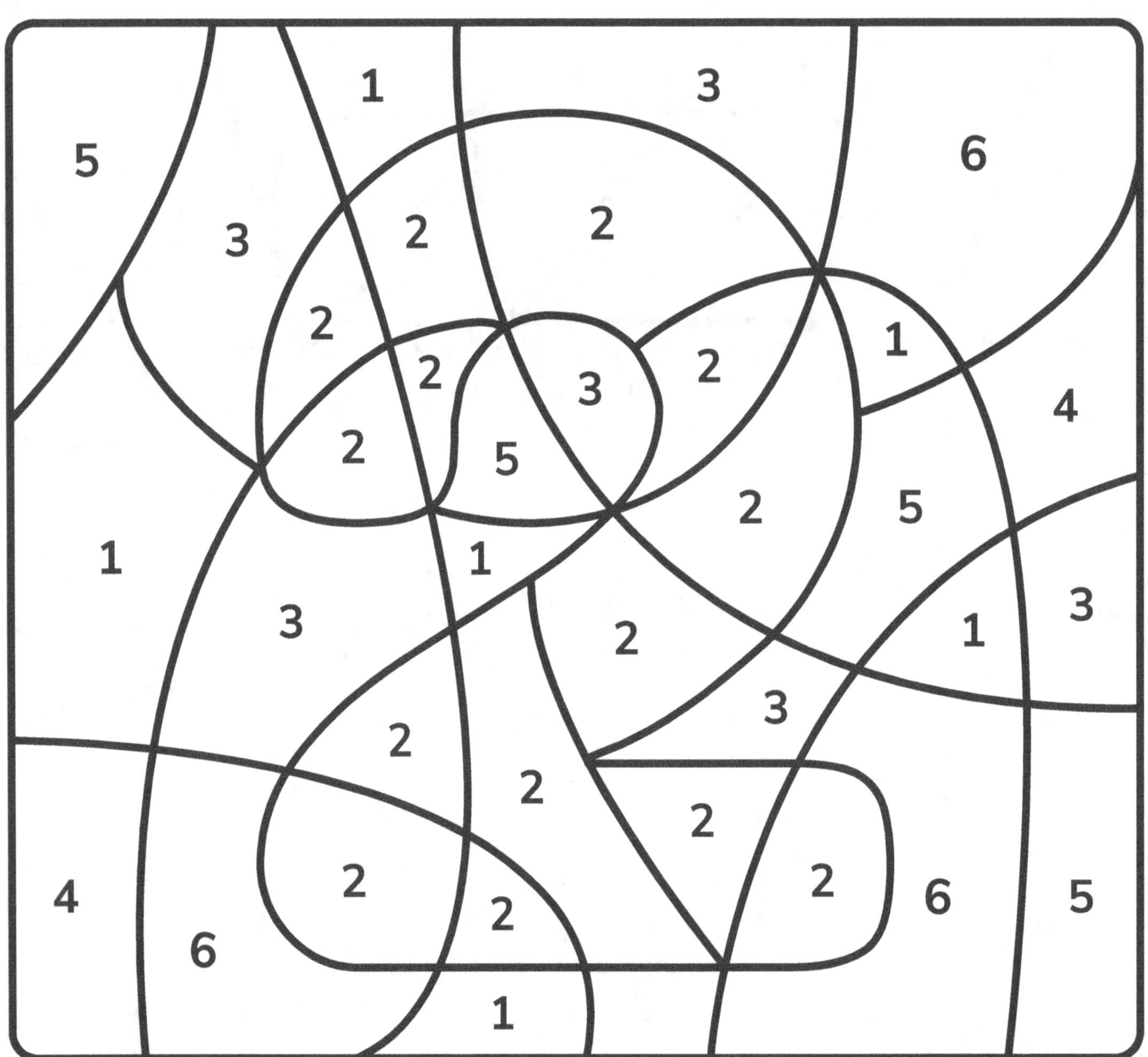

Place the number of the picture in the box below then write it out.

Find the number

Color in all the cells that have the number 9 to reveal a picture.

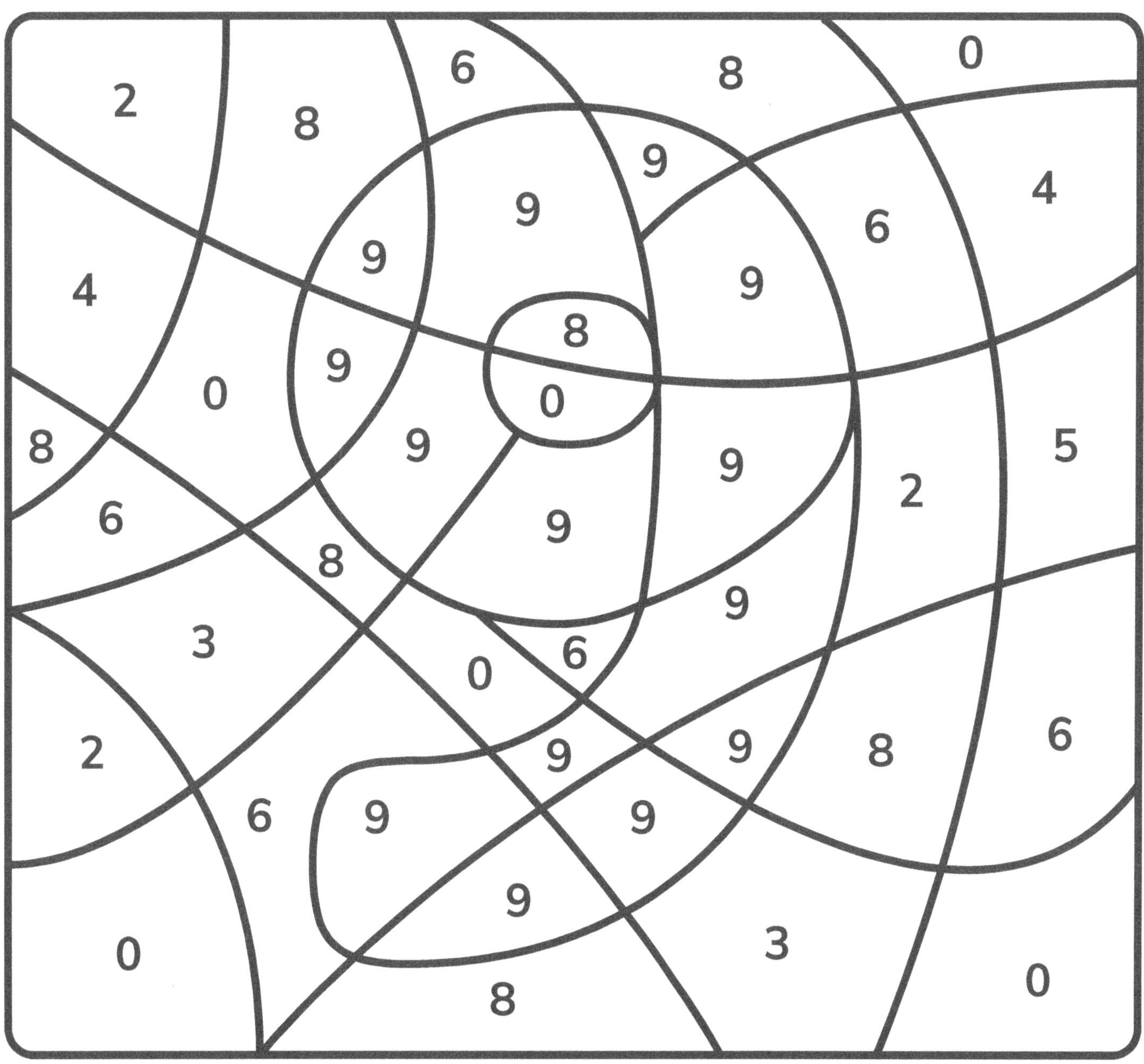

Place the number of the picture in the box below then write it out.

Find the number

Color in all the cells that have the number **6** to reveal a picture.

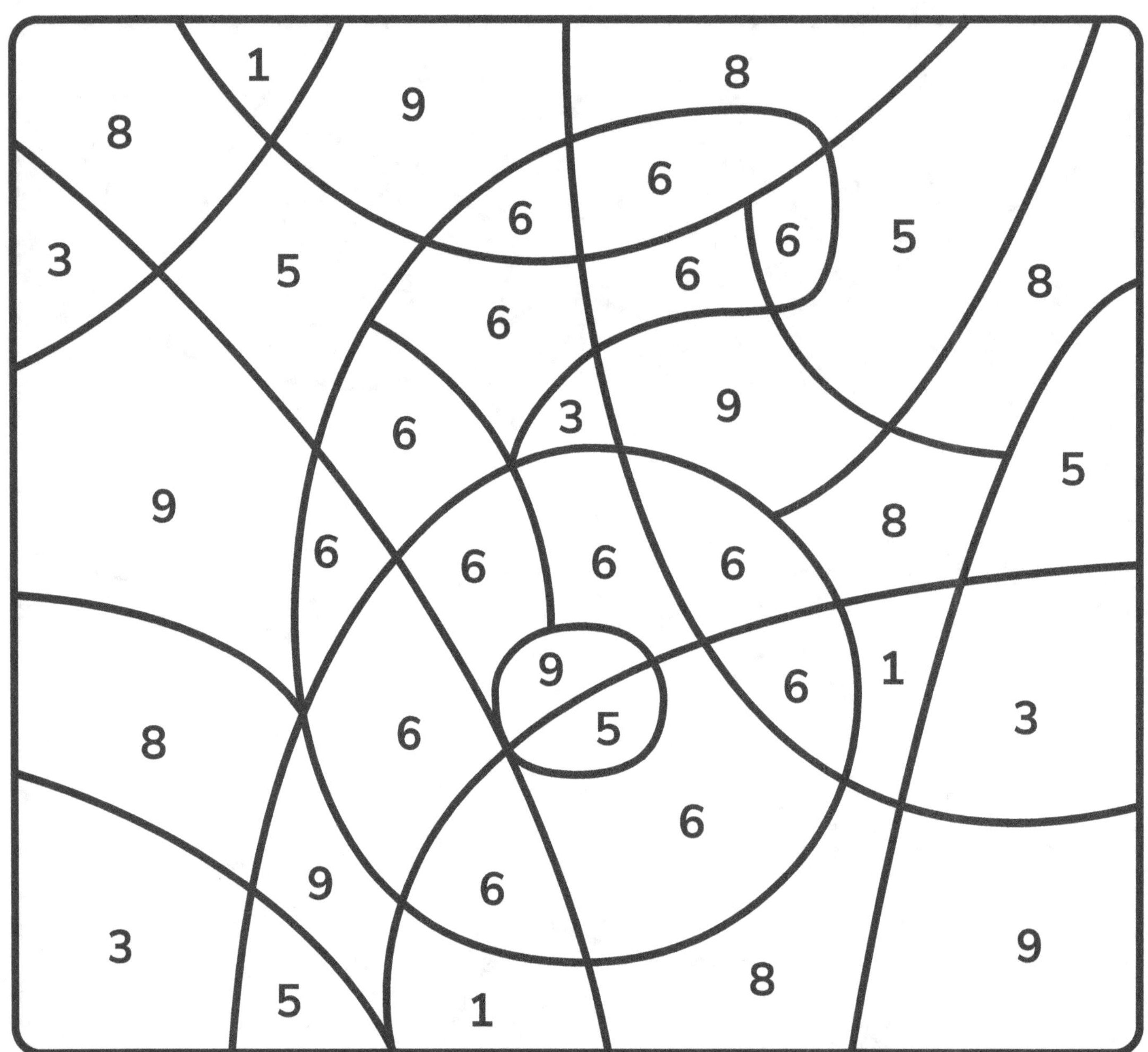

Place the number of the picture in the box below then write it out.

Find the number

Color in all the cells that have the number 3 to reveal a picture.

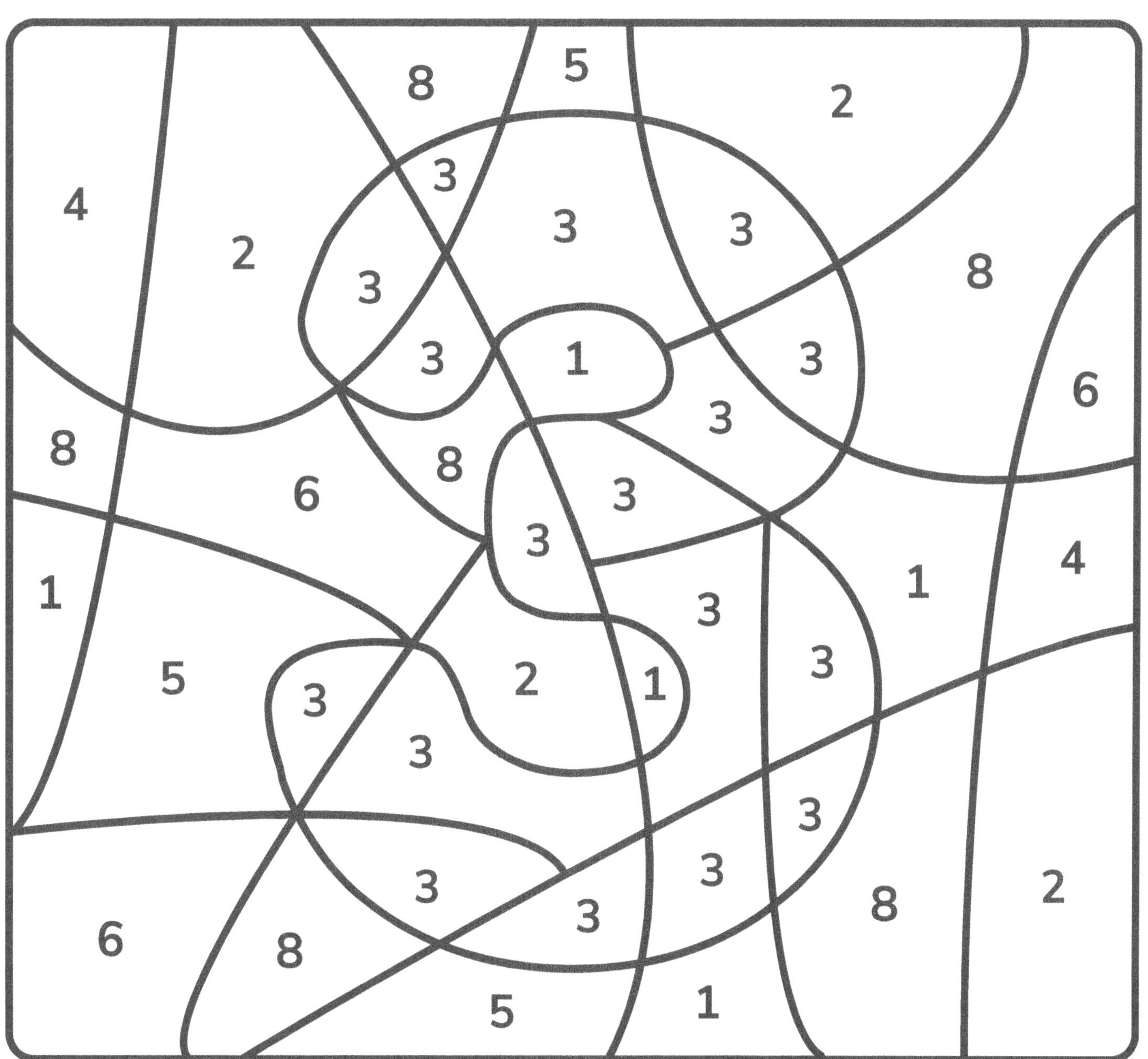

Place the number of the picture in the box below then write it out.

Find the number

Color in all the cells that have the number 4 to reveal a picture.

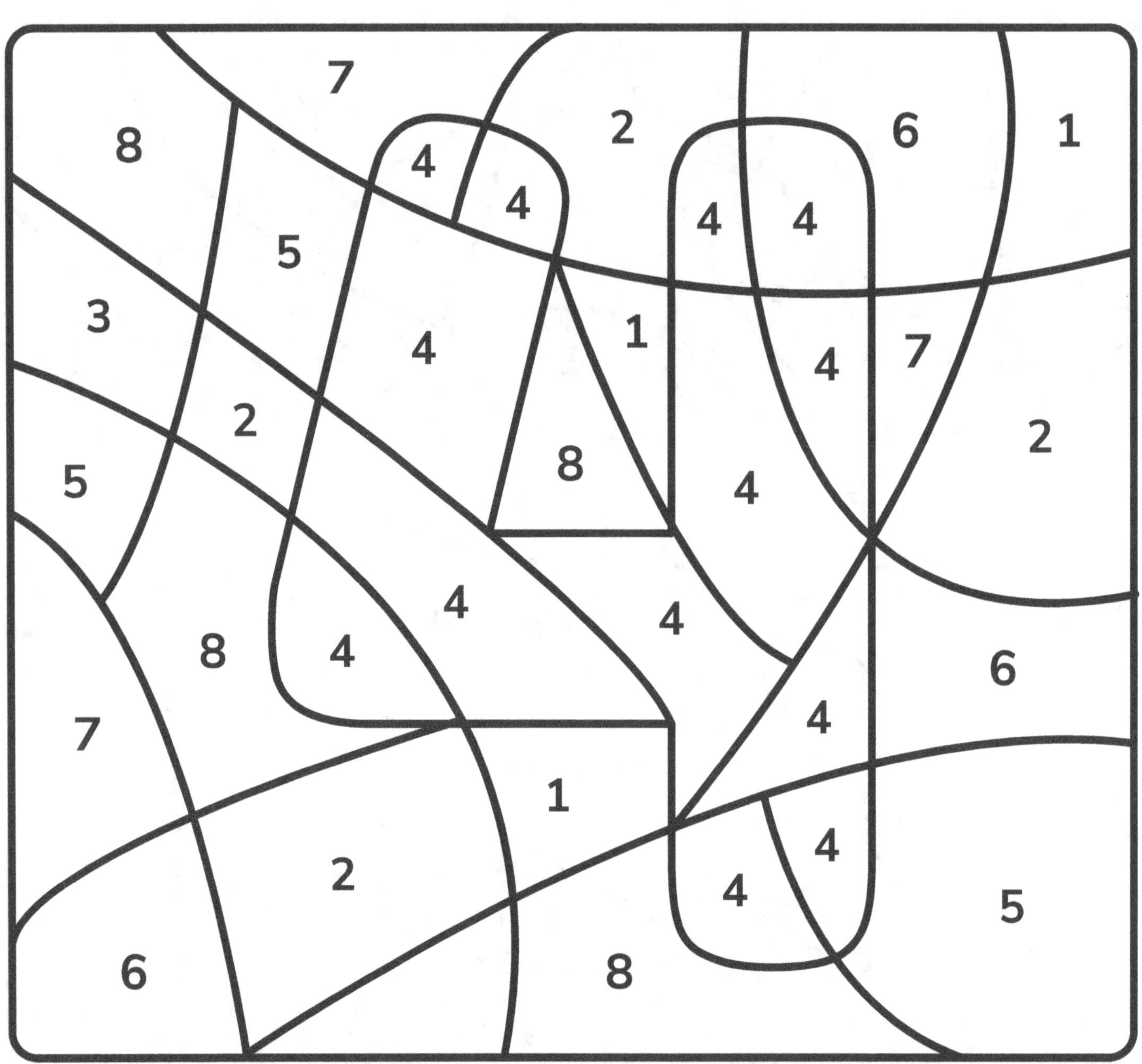

Place the number of the picture in the box below then write it out.

Find the number

Color in all the cells that have the number 1 to reveal a picture.

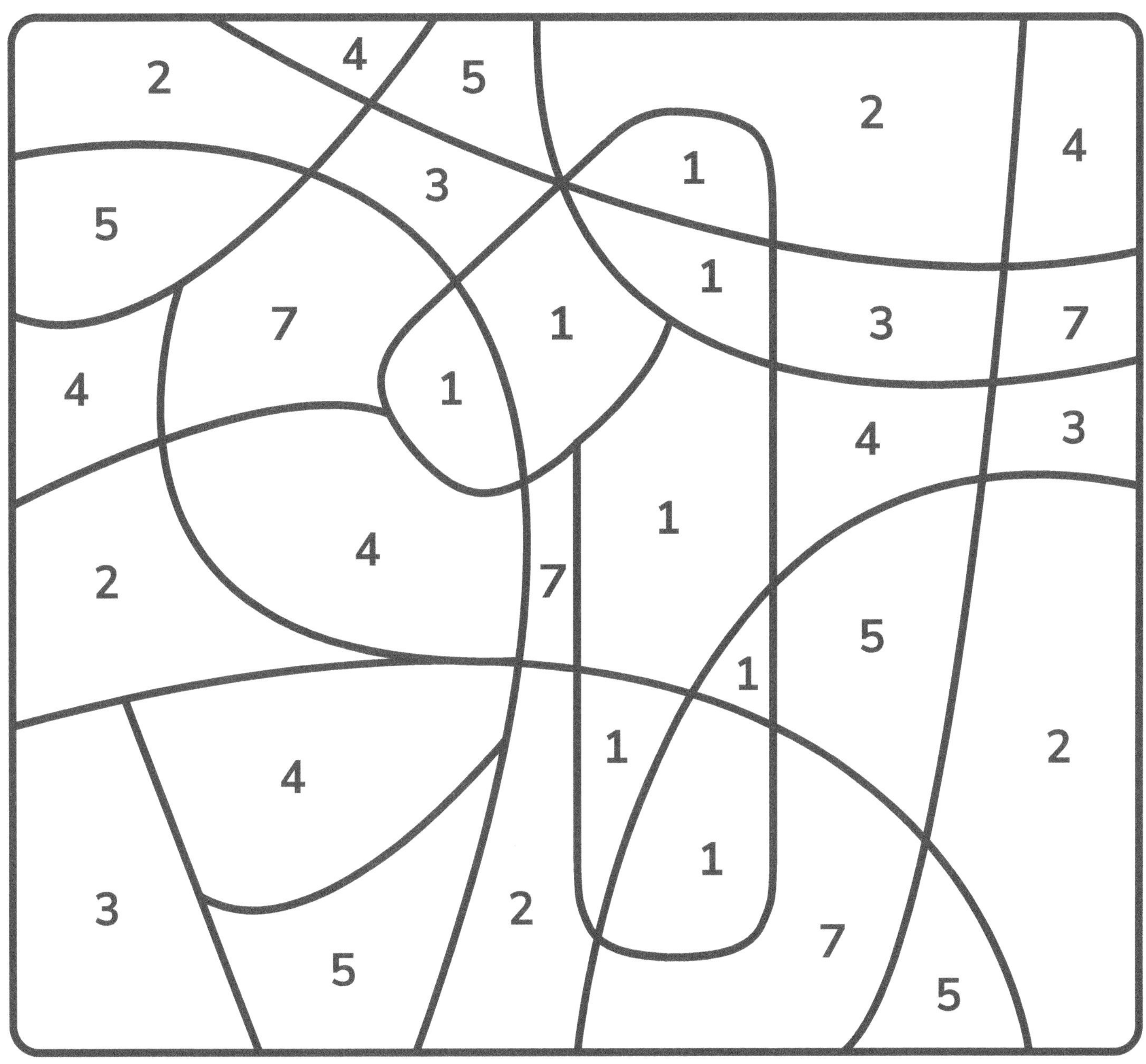

Place the number of the picture in the box below then write it out.

Find the number

Color in all the cells that have the number **5** to reveal a picture.

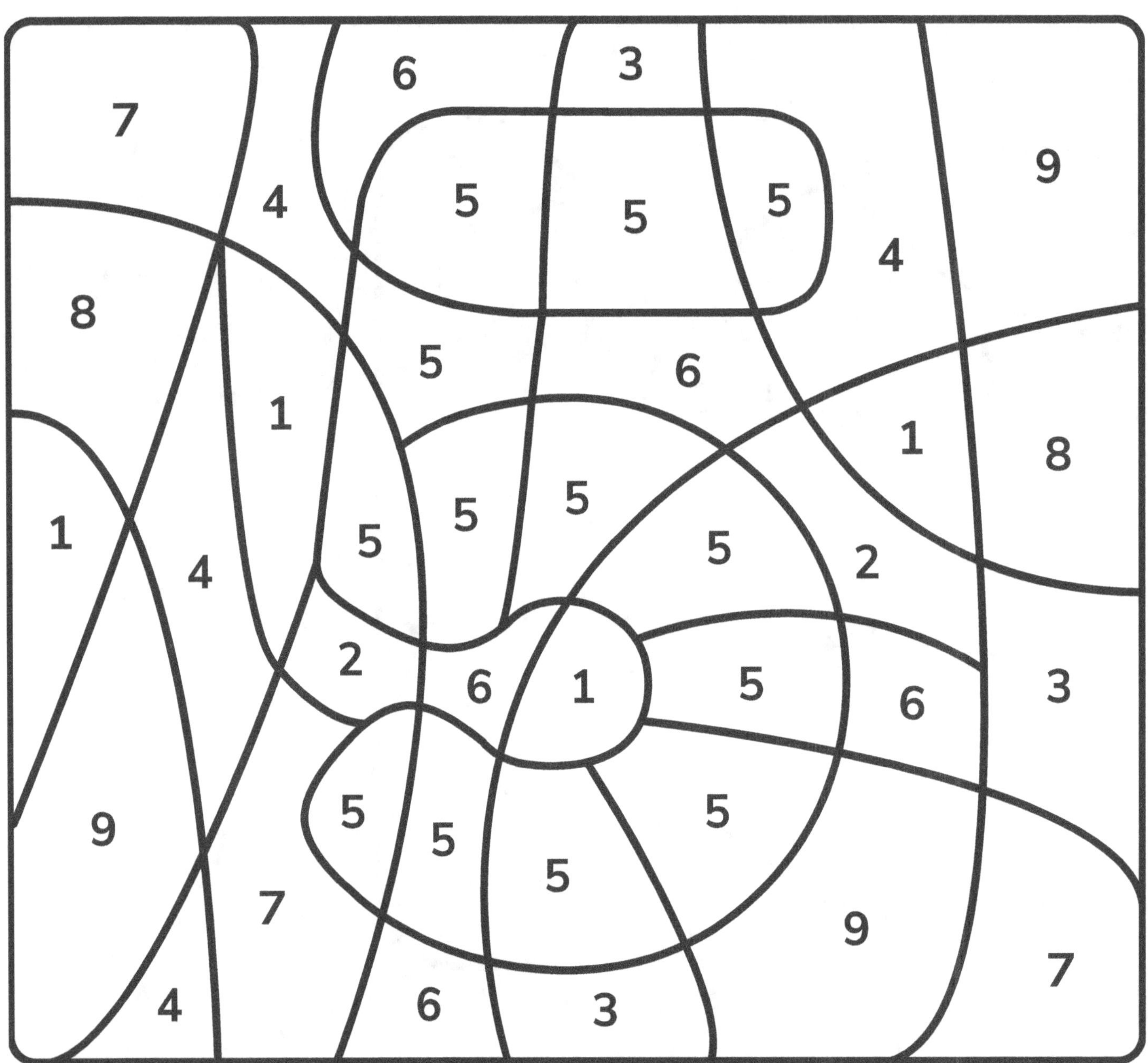

Place the number of the picture in the box below then write it out.

Find the number

Color in all the cells that have the number 10 to reveal a picture.

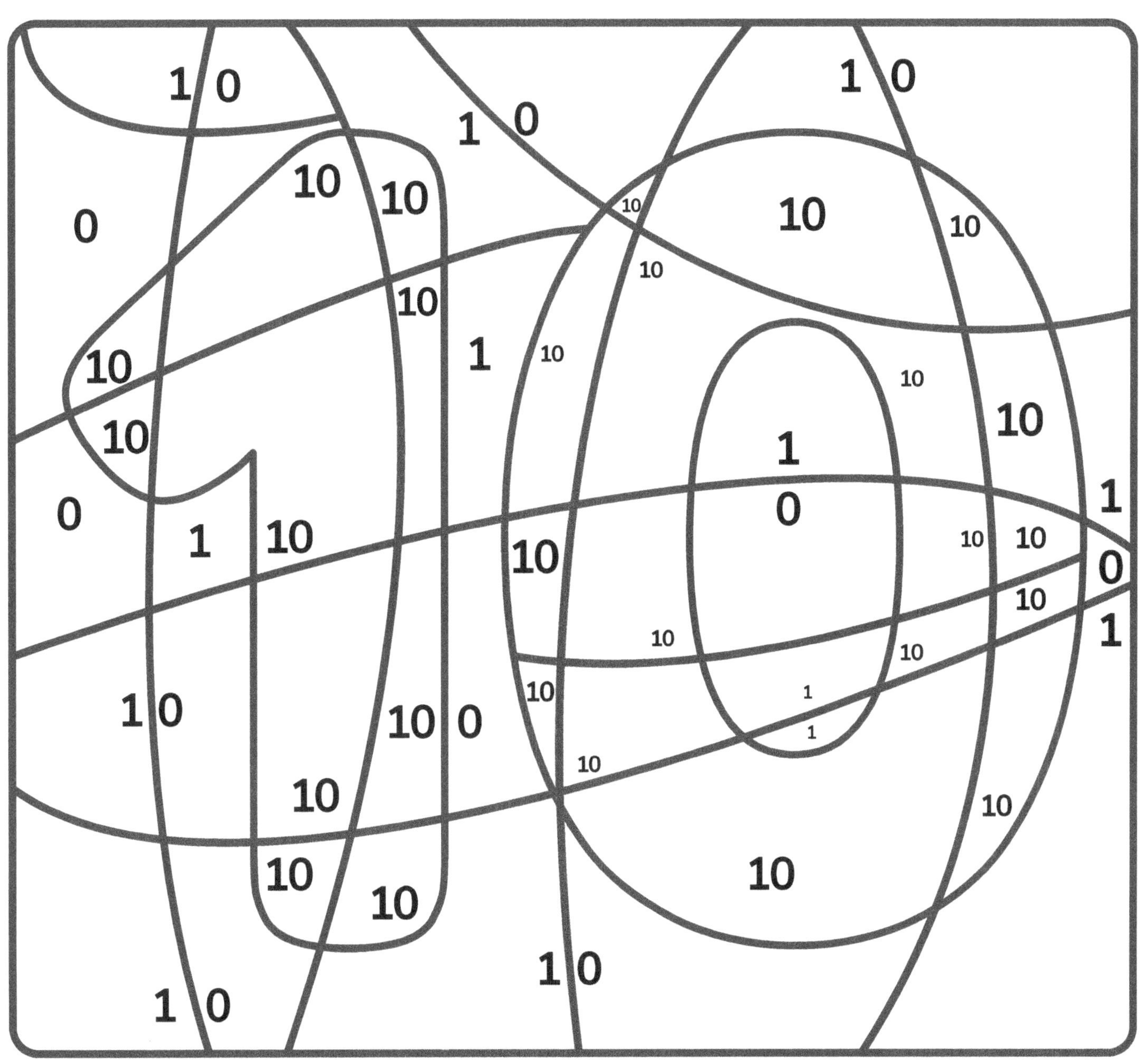

Place the number of the picture in the box below then write it out.

Congratulatons on completeing Learn To Write Numbers!

Send us an email to: **hello@edukidspress.com** with the title: *Learn To Write Numbers& Shapes* and tell us your **name** and we will email you back a Certificate of Completion in color with your name printed on it and some surprises!

Tracing and Learning Shapess

IIn this section, children will learn about the characteristics of ten basic geometric shapes: rhombuses, triangles, rectangles, squares, circles, trapezoids, pentagons, hexagons, stars, and hearts.

Learning to distinguish different shapes is an important math readiness skill; this workbook will help your child develop this skill, using a number of fun activities. Soon your young learner will be identifying shapes in all kinds of everyday objects!

It's not necessary to complete all pages in one sitting, although each page should be completed before going on to the next. The child should complete each page at their own pace and, ideally, with the encouragement and engagement of an adult.

Trace the name of the shape, then say it aloud.

circle

Trace both of the circles below. Pay close attention to the arrows

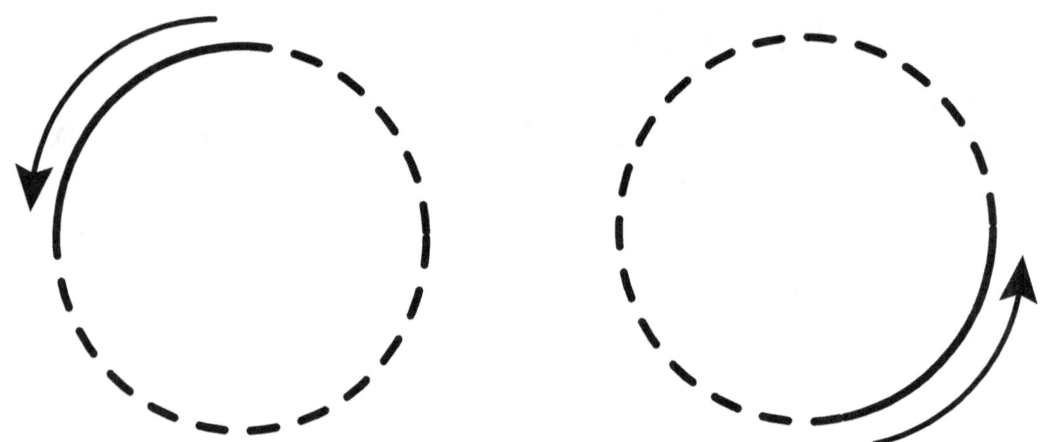

Circles come in different sizes. Trace all the circles below.

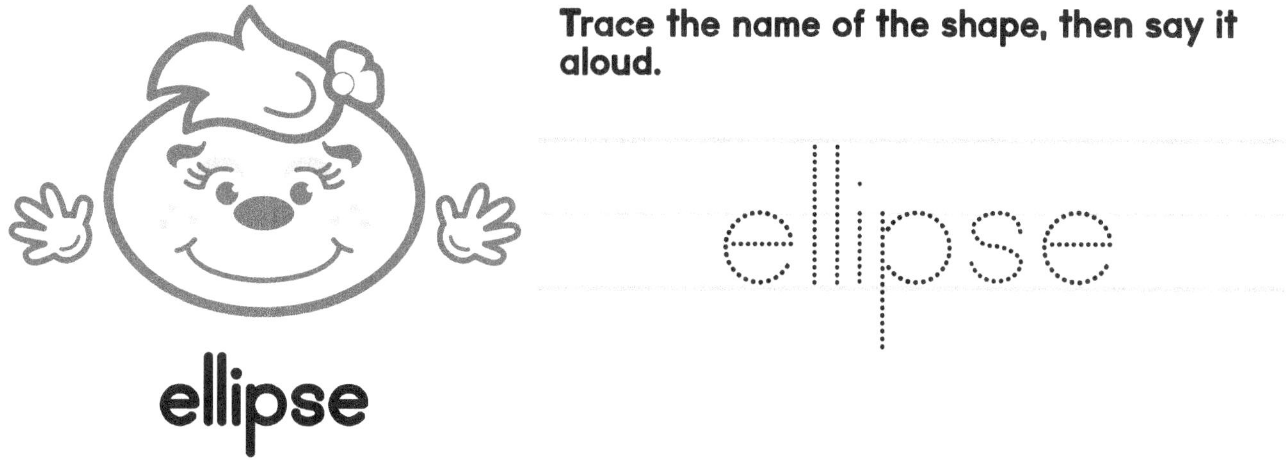

Trace both of the ellipses below. Pay close attention to the arrows

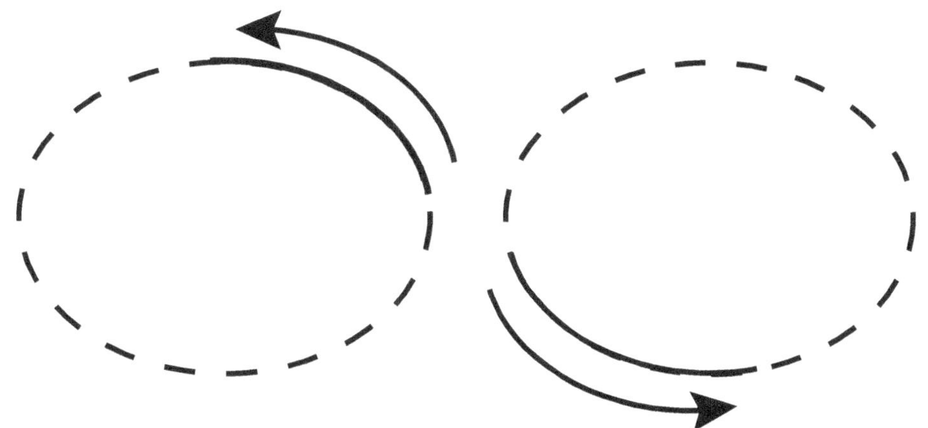

Ellipse come in all sizes but always have 2 sides the same. Trace them all

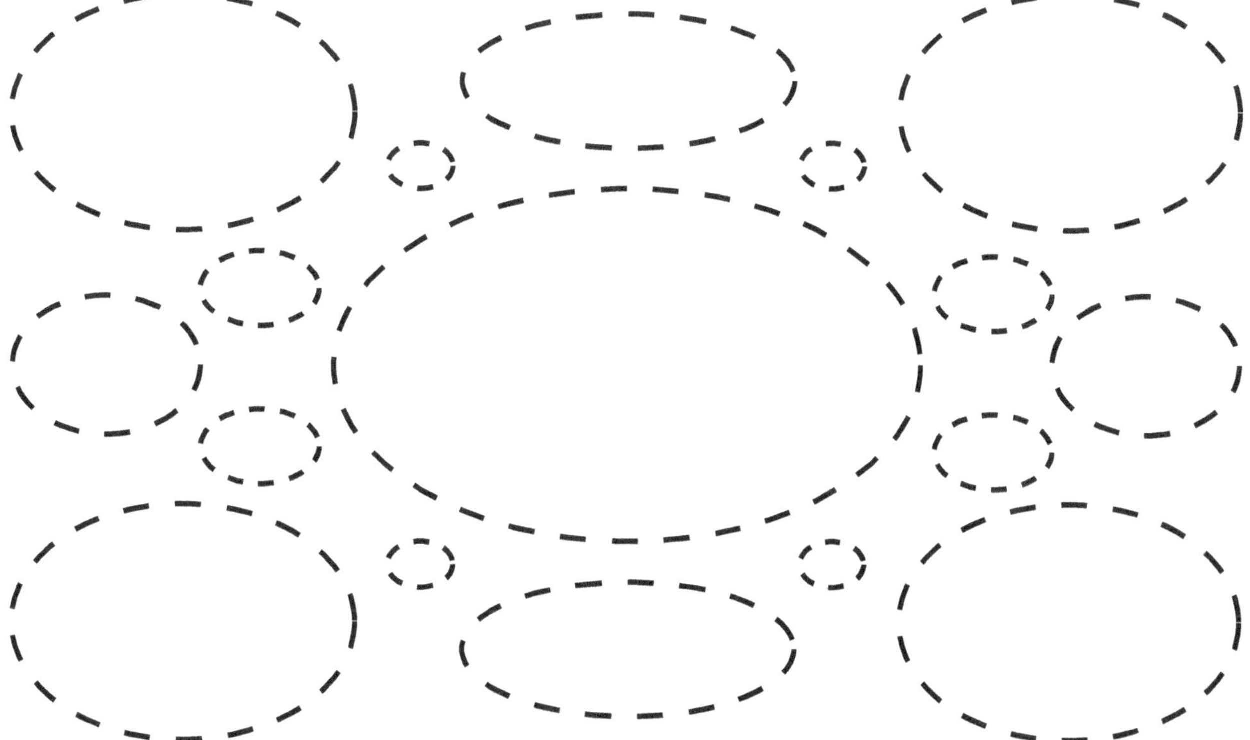

Trace the name of the shape, then say it aloud.

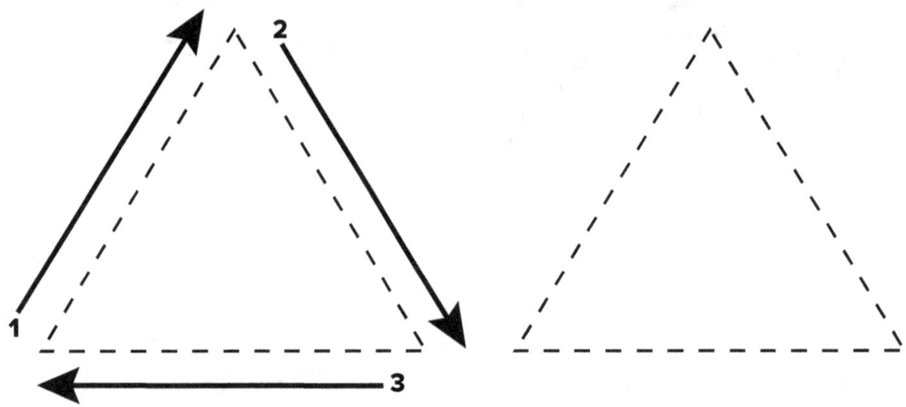

A triangle has 3 sides and 3 angles.
An angle is the space formed when 2 lines meet each other.

Trace both of the triangles below. Pay close attention to the arrows

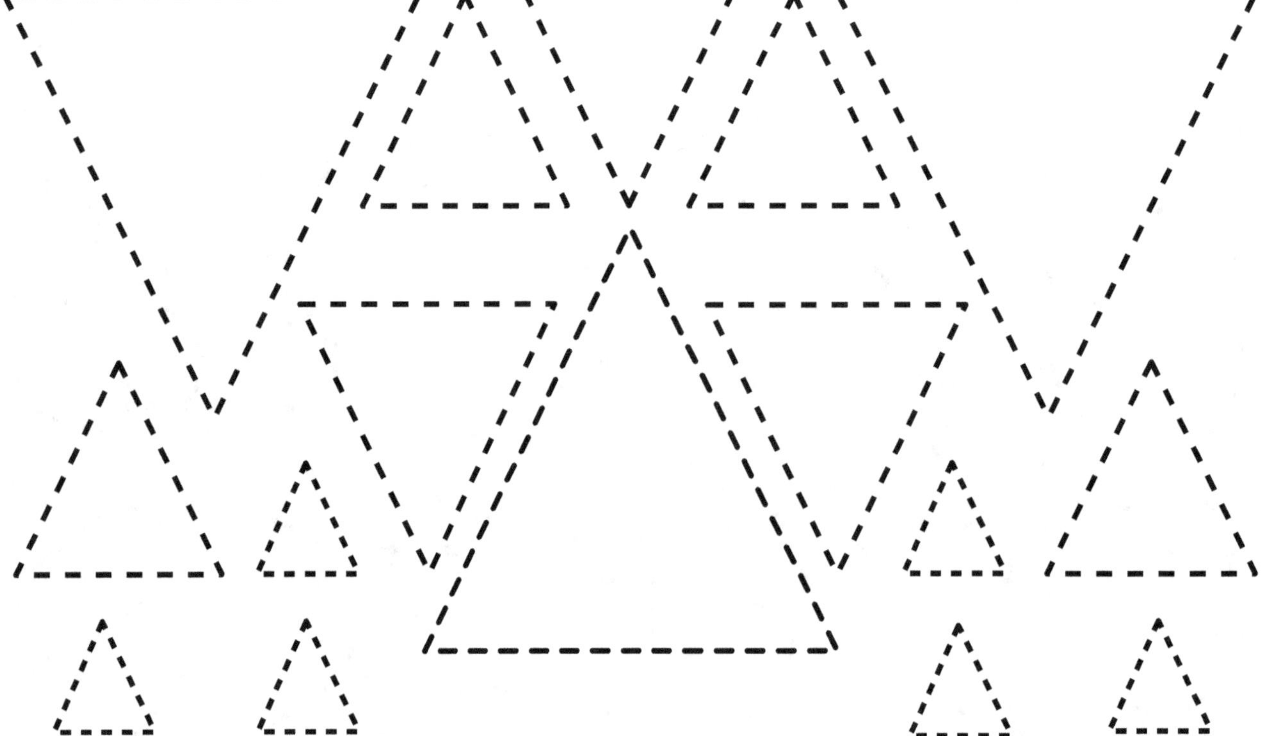

Triangles come in different sizes. Trace all the triangles below.

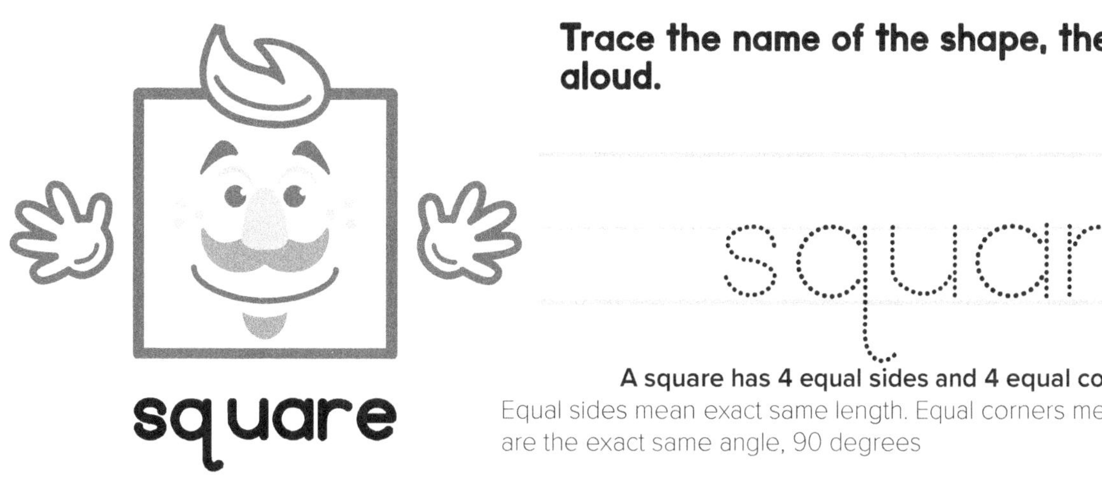

Trace the name of the shape, then say it aloud.

A square has 4 equal sides and 4 equal corners.
Equal sides mean exact same length. Equal corners mean the corners are the exact same angle, 90 degrees

Trace the squares below. Pay close attention to the arrows

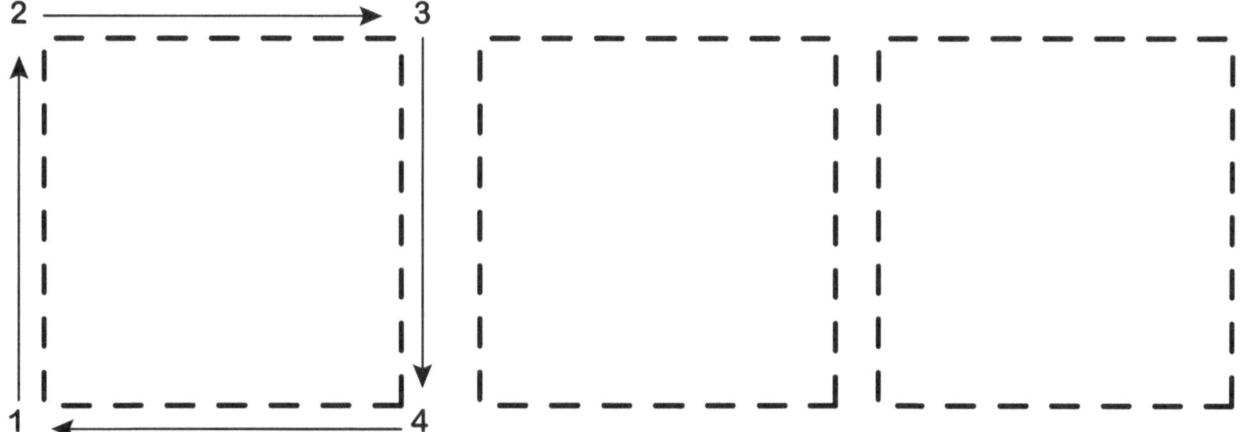

Squares come in all sizes but always have 4 sides the same. Trace them all

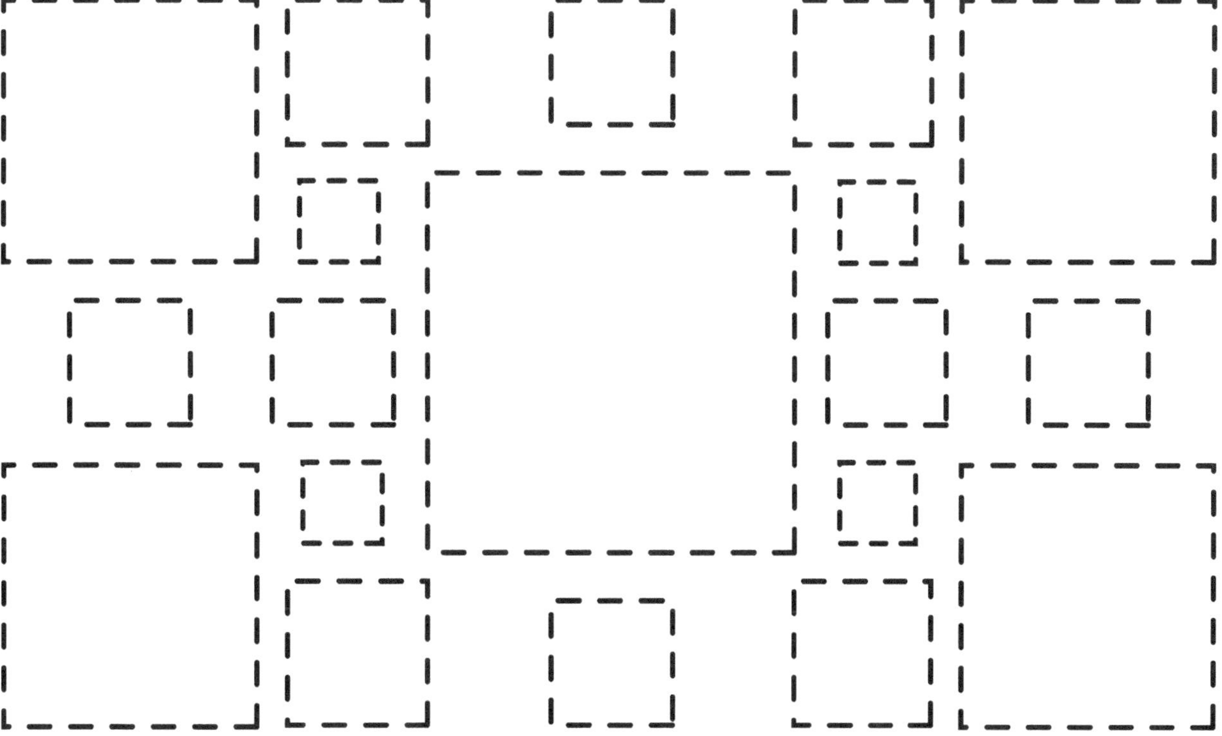

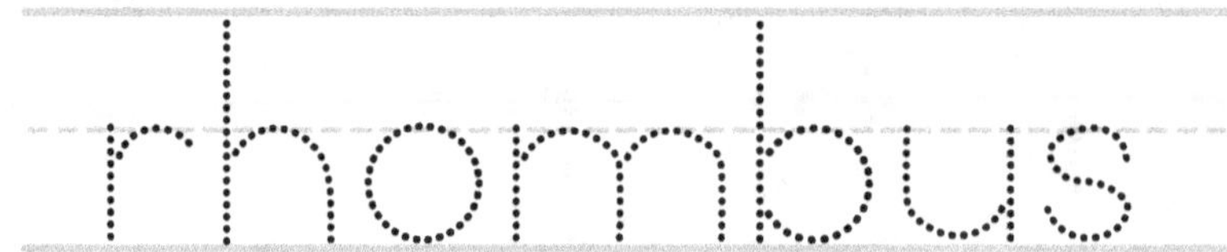

Trace the rhombus below. Pay close attention to the arrows

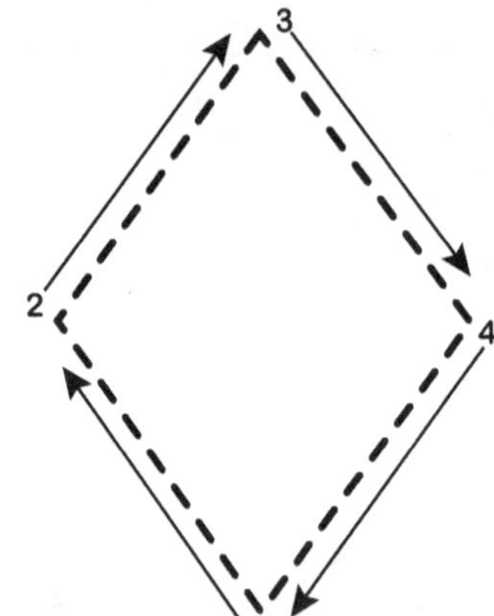

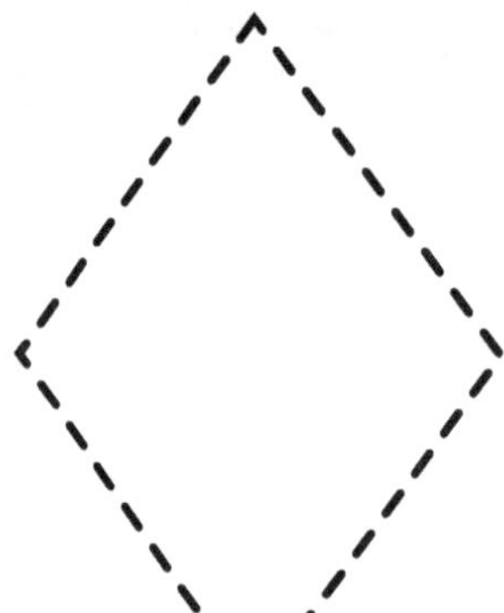

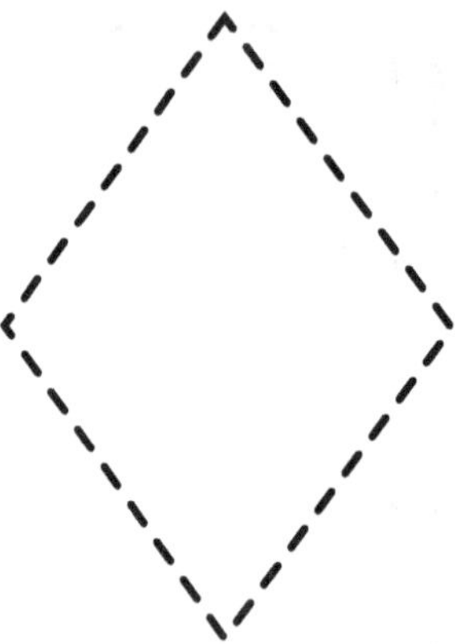

Rhombus come in different sizes . Trace all the rhonbuses below.

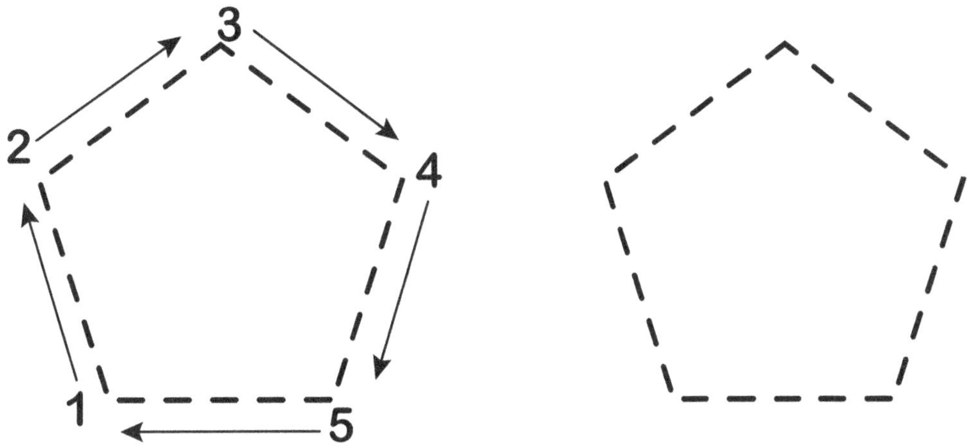

Trace both of the pentagons below. Pay close attention to the arrows

Pentagons always have 5 equal sides. Trace them all

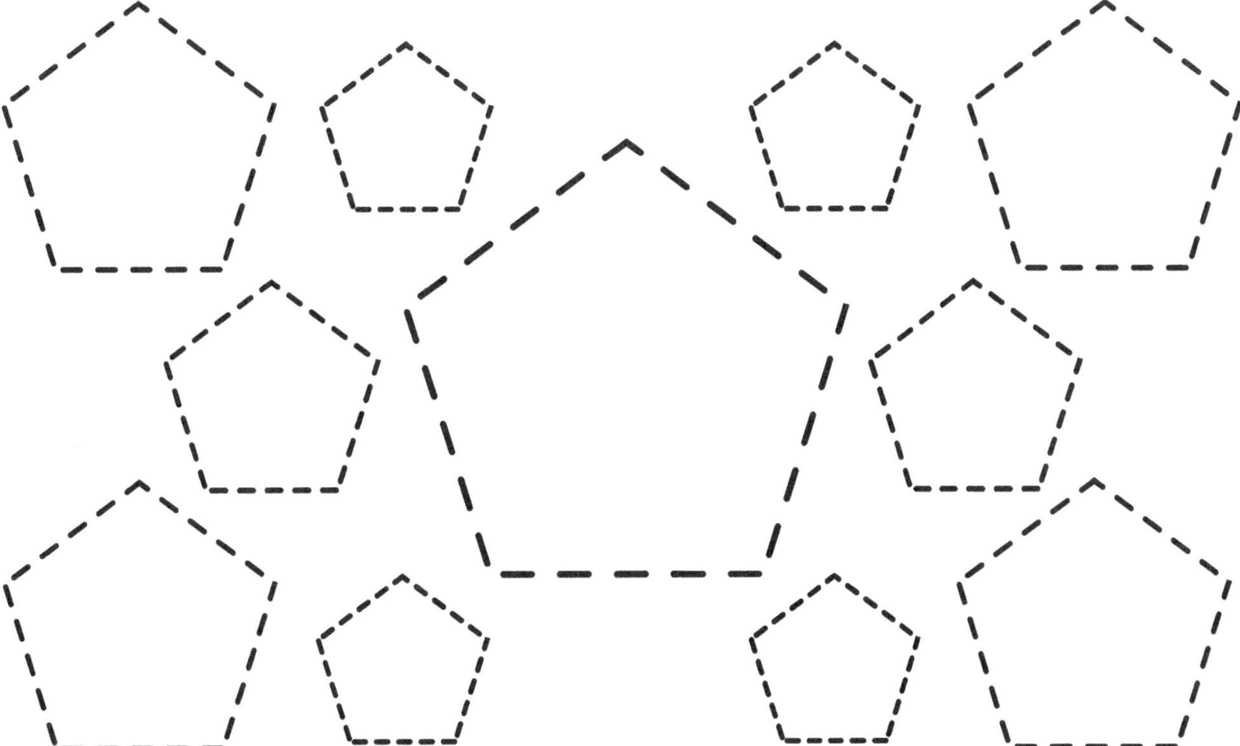

rectangle

Trace both of the triangles below. Pay close attention to the arrows

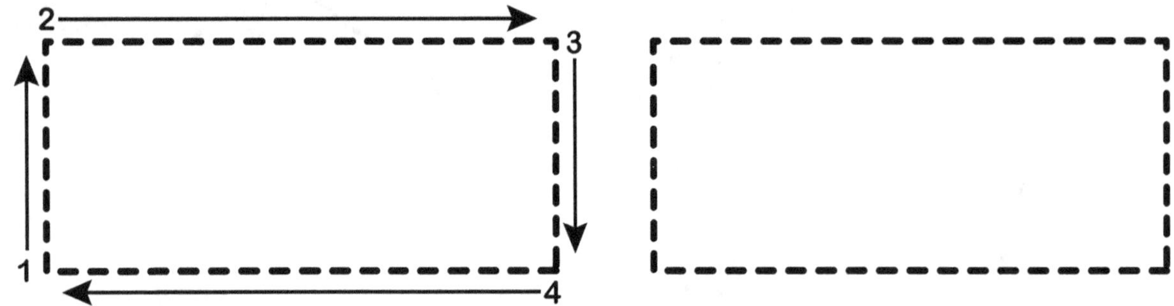

Rectangles come in different sizes. Trace all rectangles below.

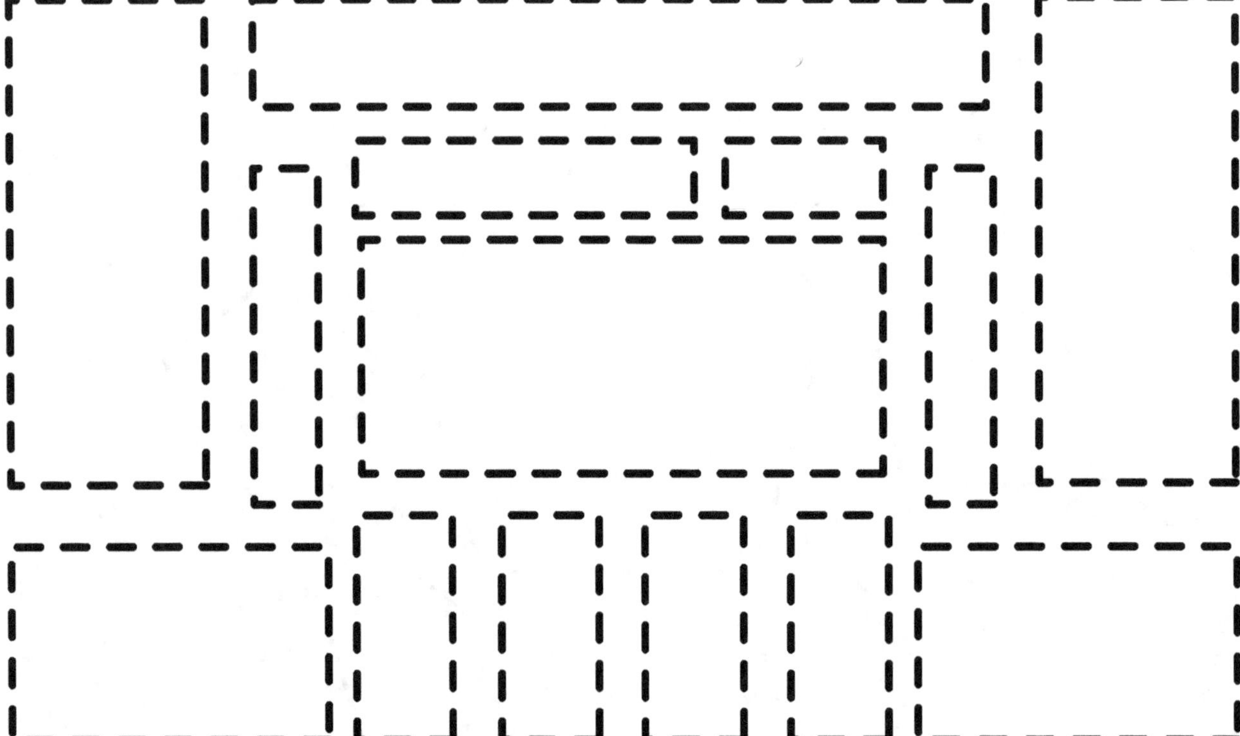

Trace the name of the shape, then say it aloud.

Trace both of the trapezoids below. Pay close attention to the arrows

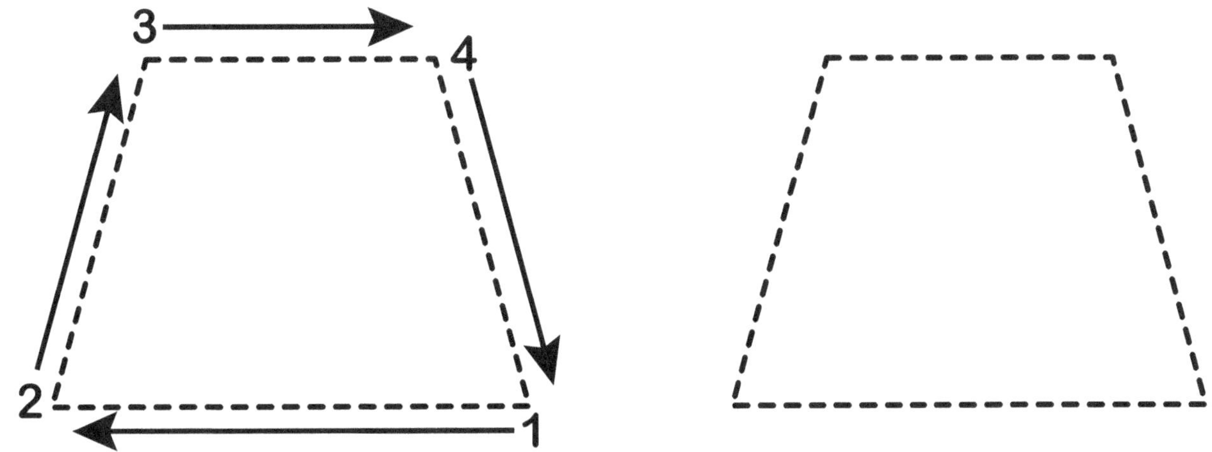

Trapezoids come in all sizes but always have 4 sides the same. Trace them.

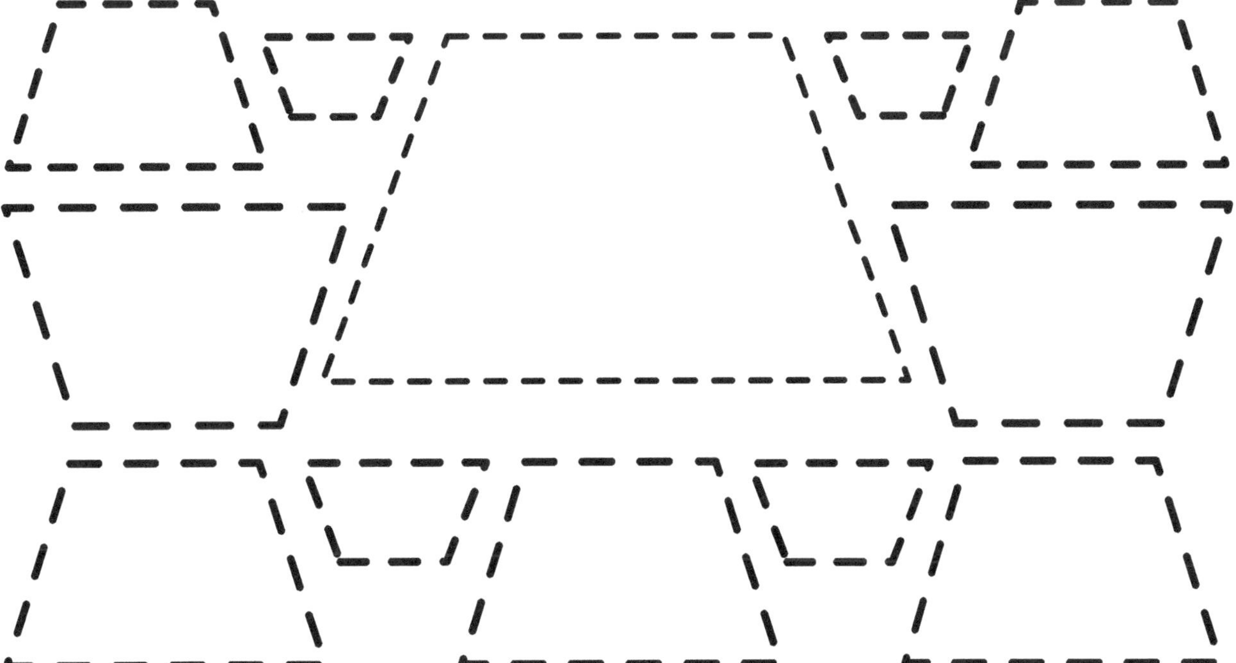

Trace the name of the shape, then say it aloud.

heart

Trace both of the hearts below. Pay close attention to the arrows

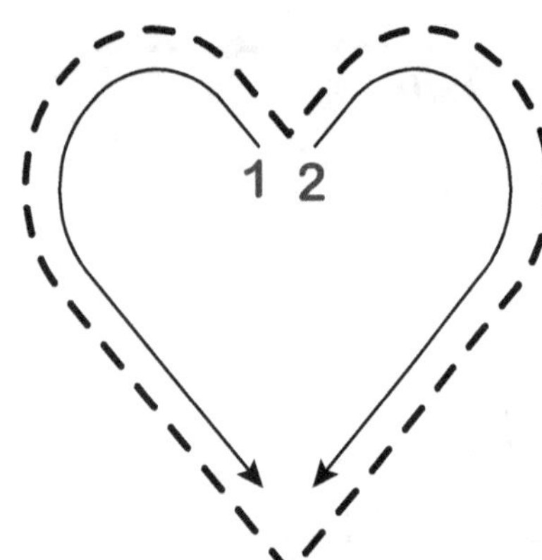

Hearts come in different shapes and sizes. Trace all the Hearts below.

Trace the name of the shape, then say it aloud.

Follow the steps and trace to make a star. Pay close attention to the arrows

| Make a mountain | Make a diagonal line | Make a line across the mountian | Make a diagonal line to connect |

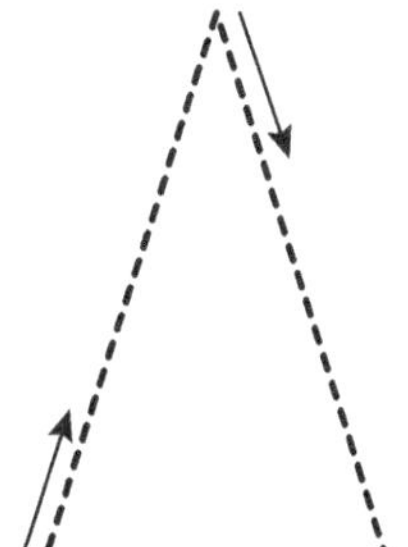 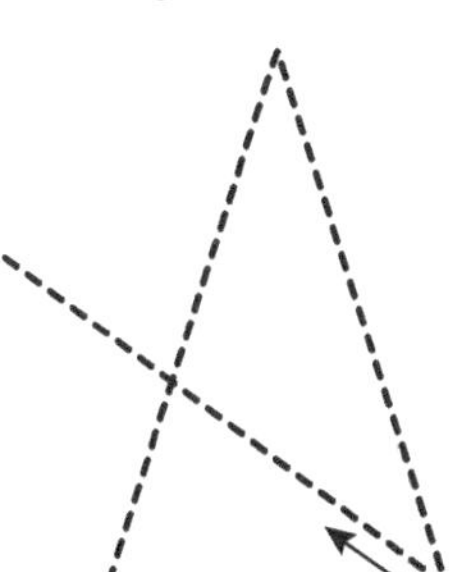 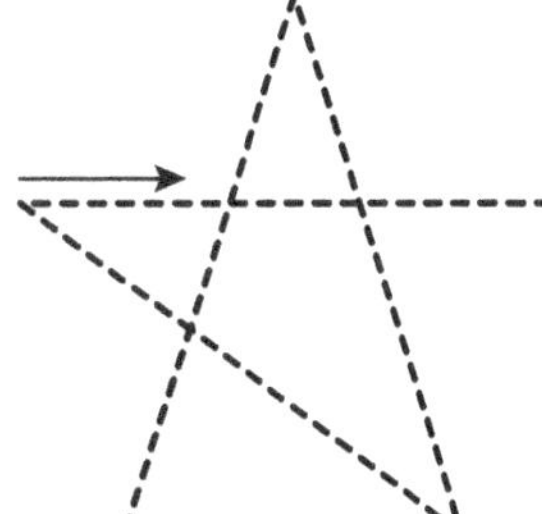 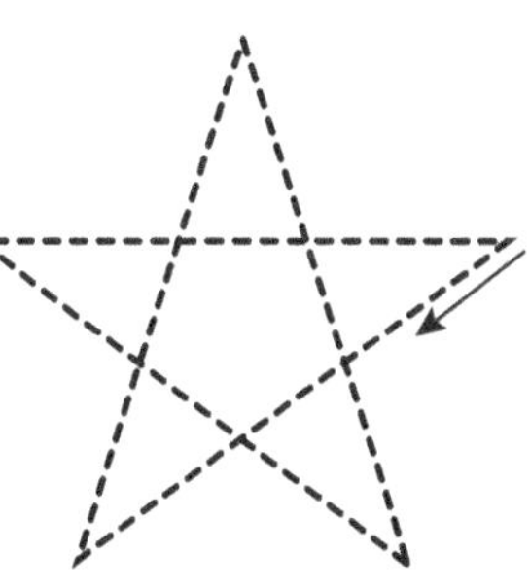

Trace the 5-pointed star polygons below.

What shape am I?

Draw a line from the shape to the correct name

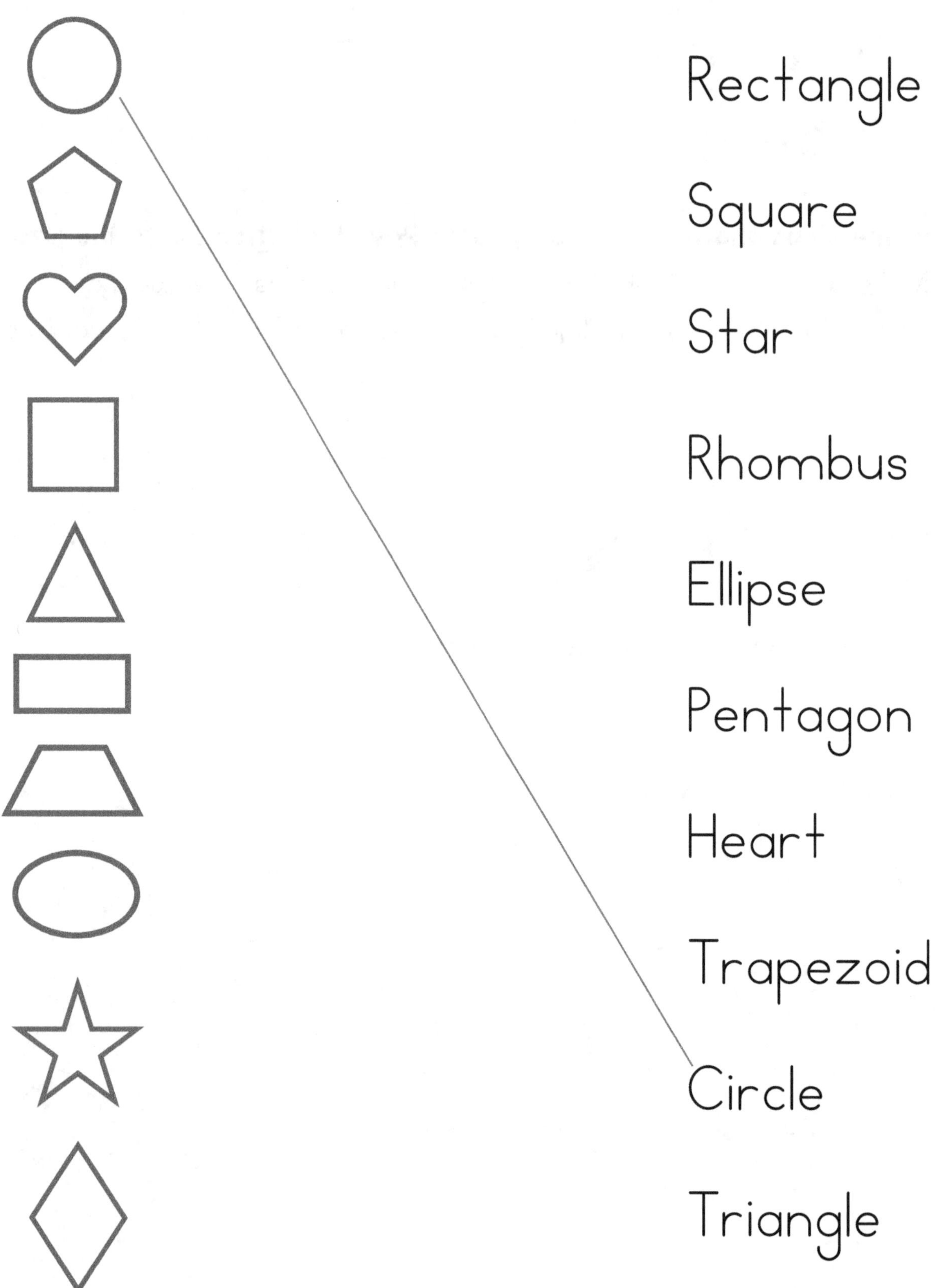

On the following pages use the fun shape at the top of each page as a guide to practice drawing shapes. You can add a face to the shape if you like. Then color in all the shapes.

Have Fun!

Hi! I'm a circle.
Draw and color
me below.

Hi! I'm a ellipse. Draw and color me below.

Hi! I'm a triangle. Draw and color me below.

Hi! I'm a square.
Draw and color
me below.

Hi! I'm a rhombus. Draw and color me below.

Hi! I'm a pentagon. Draw and color me below.

Hi! I'm a rectangle. Draw and color me below.

Hi! I'm a trapezoid. Draw and color me below.

Hi! I'm a heart.
Draw and color
me below.

Hi! I'm a star.
Draw and color
me below

Practice writing out numerals and numbers in words. Use the page to the right as a guide.

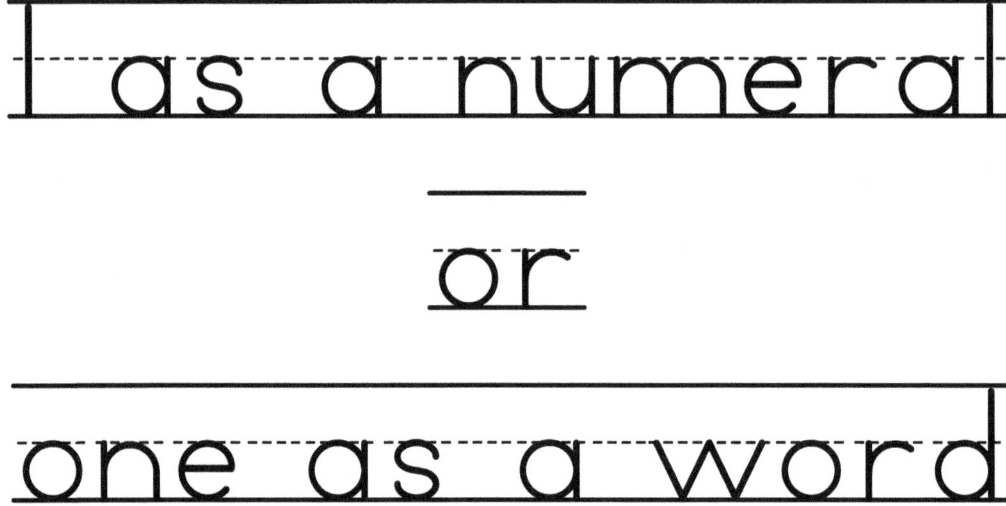

1 or one

2 or two

3 or three

4 or four

5 or five

6 or six

7 or seven

8 or eight

9 or nine

10 or ten

Notes

Notes

See our other handwriting workbooks at:

http://bit.ly/EduKidsPress

ALPHABET HANDWRITING PRACTICE LEARN TO WRITE WORKBOOK

KINDERGARTEN WRITING PAPER WITH LINES FOR ABC KIDS WORKBOOK

Thank you for using this workbook! Please take a moment to review it on Amazon; we read every review and your feedback will help us develop future workbooks.

Want to stay updated with news about our books?
Visit: www.edukidspress.com

SEE ALL OF OUR BOOKS AT:
http://bit.ly/EduKidsPress

EDU KIDS PRESS